# John Hudson

# Christmas 1914

## The First World War At Home and Abroad

*In memory of Private John Rigby Foy,*
*12th Battalion, The King's (Liverpool Regiment)*
*who died in Northern France, 2 June 1918*

First published 2014

The History Press
The Mill, Brimscombe Port
Stroud, Gloucestershire, GL5 2QG
www.thehistorypress.co.uk

© John Hudson, 2014

The right of John Hudson to be identified as the Author
of this work has been asserted in accordance with the
Copyright, Designs and Patents Act 1988.

British Library Cataloguing in Publication Data.
A catalogue record for this book is available from the British Library.

ISBN 978 0 7509 6028 1

Typesetting and origination by The History Press
Printed and bound by CPI Group (UK) Ltd, Croydon, CR0 4YY

# CONTENTS

# ACKNOWLEDGEMENTS

Thanks are due to David Glass and Bob Duckett of the Bradford Historical and Antiquarian Society; Jan Sykes of Bradford Local Studies Library; Su Holgate at Bradford Metropolitan District Council; the staff of Bristol Central Library; Stephen Dixon; Linda Hudson, for proofreading and much more; the Trustees and Documents and Sound Section of the Imperial War Museum for allowing access to the collections and to E. Morgan, copyright holder of the papers of W.M. Floyd; Cate Ludlow and Ruth Boyes of The History Press; Svetlana Palmer and Sarah Wallis for permission to use an extract from *A War In Words*, with acknowledgements to Simon and Schuster UK; Toby Pinn of Clevedon Salerooms; the staff of Stroud Library; Gillian Thomas of Treorchy Library; Phil Vasili; and the copyright holders of all quoted songs.

# INTRODUCTION

There are two facts about Christmas 1914 that are known by all and will probably be so another 100 years from now. One is that everybody believed the Great War would be over by then and festive peace would be celebrated around the home fires, and the other is that extraordinary truce, with the football kickabouts and shared sweets, Schnapps and cigarettes with 'our friend the enemy' Fritz in no-man's-land.

The truth, of course, is rather different: any realistic hopes of an early end to the war had dissipated almost within days of its outbreak. The British Expeditionary Force's first significant taste of action at the Battle of Mons had seen it inflict heavy casualties on the enemy but fail to hold the line of the Mons–Condé Canal and eventually retreat over two weeks to almost the outskirts of Paris. A straightforward tactical retreat executed in good order, the top brass explained. To the British press, however, yet to be properly reminded that truth is the first casualty of war, it was a humiliating and bitter disaster; a bravely fought disaster, granted, but a disaster for all that.

When our troops again came face to face with the German First Army, at the River Marne east of Paris, it was still only early September. This time, however, the French, whose tactical withdrawal at Mons had unwittingly helped to put the British forces in an impossible position, were everything an ally should be in their fierce defence of their capital, and the Kaiser's hopes of a swift victory on the Western Front came to nothing. Instead, his army retreated to the north east, the British and French pursued it and both sides then showed they had learned lessons from the way they had been conducting themselves to date by digging deep trenches and settling in for the long, long haul. Any brave talk of victory by Christmas – and in truth, both sides had at first been dreaming that dream – soon foundered in the mud of Flanders.

Trench warfare was not unknown in military history, but it was not what the British public had foreseen; they were far more familiar with the concept of fast-moving, fluid battle lines, and while the retreat from Mons was the last thing they wanted to see in the way of fluidity, at least they understood the scenario. Trench warfare? Idle men peeping over the parapet and eyeballing the equally indolent and inactive enemy? To some armchair generals back at home by their firesides there was almost something comical about it.

We can see, then, that it had been determined some months before the event that Christmas 1914 would not be a peacetime celebration; and developments leading immediately up to it, that December, saw such an escalation in hostilities that any hopes of a happier New Year were now equally forlorn. Already the newspapers were dominated by war news, and tributes to bewildering numbers of young men who were losing their lives on the other side of the English Channel. This was particularly disorienting and distressing in the local weekly press, whose pages hitherto had rarely been sullied by troubles any more disturbing than the police court sequels to fights outside the Dog and Duck on Saturday nights. December, however, was the month when 'Over There' became

The trenches as a somewhat comical curiosity: this postcard did not appear again after that first Christmas of war. (Author's collection)

'Over Here', and that was a backward step by no means everybody had reckoned with.

It started in the middle of the month and swiftly escalated; a bag of what looked to be rusty rivets was dropped on Southend; on the 15th the first Zeppelin was sighted off the east coast – and as these had long been supposed to pose Germany's main threat from the air, were such an outlandish proposition possible at all, that seemed an ominous sign; not nearly so ominous, however, as the events of the following morning, when German battleships were left free to bombard the north-east coastal towns of the Hartlepools, Scarborough and Whitby, killing well over 100 defenceless men, women and children. At the same time, one of their flotillas was sowing mines off Filey which accounted for hundreds more lives before they were cleared. There were clearly questions to be faced by the British Grand Fleet, questions rarely if ever asked in living memory as our ships 'Ruled the Waves'.

The action quickened considerably in the last days leading up to Christmas. On 21 December a German seaplane, as distinct from an airship, dropped two bombs just off Dover Harbour, and three days later one landed on the town itself, breaking a lot of windows and blowing a gardener out of a holly tree. It was the first airborne bomb to land on British soil, and although its end result was almost comical, like something out of the latest Keystone Cops film, its implications were not, with the engineering might of the Ruhr gearing

The Christmas Spirit 1914, as seen in the *New York World* by Rollin Kirby, who won the first Pulitzer Prize for Editorial Cartooning in 1922 and repeated the feat twice more in a career that spanned both world wars. (*The War Budget*, 16 January 1915)

up for the battle ahead. The first Zeppelin raid came on 19 January 1915, but airships as a fighting force were quickly made obsolete by fast-advancing technology, as were those aircraft that dealt the earliest blows of the war. On both sides of the Channel, hostility was the very fertile mother of invention.

And then came Christmas Day, that time of sharing pictures of wives and girlfriends with the foe and exchanging verses of 'Silent Night' one with another; up to a point. It was also the day of Britain's first air raid on Germany, where seaplanes did what they were able in stormy skies over Cuxhaven. The enemy were doing likewise over London Docks and the Medway towns, while those mines planted in the North Sea nine days earlier were blowing ships out of the water with distressing loss of life. Even on the Western Front, all was far from quiet in most areas: men were still fighting and dying; in some trenches, the enemy was passive, so the other side stayed passive, too; there was 'gardening' to be done on no-man's–land, burying bodies, clearing weapons and debris, and spasmodic local arrangements were made for this to be carried out by both sides without fear of aggression. Anything over and above this was the exception; so exceptional, in fact, that it is still recalled with awe to this day. The other fact everyone knows about it is that it never happened again.

The aim of this book, as its title suggests, is to give a rounded account of life in Britain at or around

Christmas 1914, by far the strangest Christmas everyone who lived through it had ever known. Apart from the conflict, and the toll it was taking on families' menfolk and morale, there were so many other life-changing developments to take in and digest: the sudden need for women in the workplace, quiet towns that had been transformed into part of the war machine by creating arms and weapons, young men who had not enlisted for whatever reason being constantly harried to do so, the patriotic need for a recently volatile workforce to buckle down, the wounded soldiers in the streets and parks, the refugees from Belgium and elsewhere who were now a part of our local communities, with all the civic responsibilities that implied.

On New Year's Day the editor of a small West Country weekly newspaper wrote:

> A stranger and duller sort of Christmas could hardly be imagined ... The awful anxieties and grief of war touched the whole country very closely, and in our district there was little of the usual festivities and jollity. There were no attractions beyond the local variety theatres, and whatever Christmas parties there were were quiet, while the town was in the evenings completely deserted. The weather was, on the whole, wet and dreary ... There were few visitors this year, and no engagements to interest them, while the customary list of football matches dwindled down to one or two games ...

Yet in other ways, life went on. As the above report hints, the music halls were still churning out their songs and their jokes, although at first the singers were wrapping themselves in the red, white and blue and the humour was taking on a spiky, we shall overcome feel. Soon enough, it would be back to normal with the cheek and the chutzpah. There were still personalities to read about in the papers, even if it was only footballers taking up arms or leading ladies knitting socks for sailors. America was sending over, if not its men, then engaging songs as diverse as 'I Wonder Who's Kissing Her Now' and 'Aba Daba Honeymoon'. And yes, outside the Dog and Duck, Saturday night drunks were still punching one another on the nose.

We cannot begin to recognise a good deal of what our countrymen were going through then: the dread of the telegraph boy clicking the gate latch and knocking on the door, the previously unheard-of fear of destruction from the air, the stark fact that nobody had a new 1915 calendar saying 'This is the second year of the First World War, 1914–18, which Britain won at great cost'. Uncertainty can be a devastating enemy.

Yet what we can see is a sense of commitment and community which we now regard as essentially British, even if, to some of us, it does not seem quite so much a part of our national character 100 years on in 2014. It was this, as much as the bombs and heavy artillery, maybe even as much as the Americans and Russians, that saw us through both this world war and the next one. In 1918, while German society fell apart in hunger, discontent and near-revolution, our ancestors not only held firm but redoubled their efforts on the Home Front. Men turned their backs on safe jobs to enlist, often well above (and in some cases, below) conventional military age, and the community as a whole set aside conflicts over industrial relations, universal suffrage or the rights and wrongs of the war to put their shoulders together to the wheel.

That, however, was nearly four years down the line. Christmas 1914 had challenges of its own, and some small compensations and comforts, too. Glimpsing it now we visit another world; but one in which, because of the Great War's continuing influence on all that came after it, we can still trace far-off foreshadowings of our lives today.

# A PRESENT
# FROM A PRINCESS

A still familiar memento of Christmas 1914 is the comforts tin issued to all the Empire's serving personnel in the name of Princess Mary, the 17-year-old daughter of George V and Queen Mary. In brass embossed with a somewhat self-important classical design, it cried out to be kept as a souvenir, and that was the exact fate of hundreds of thousands of them. What we must not think, if we come across one today, is 'Ah, this must have come through the hell of the trenches to survive.' The better its condition, the more likely it is that it got no nearer to Flanders than Aldershot, Whitehall or Wellington Barracks.

The gift was organised within weeks of Christmas, meaning that many of the tins did not get out until early 1915, with a 'Victorious New Year' greeting rather than a Christmas card. An advertisement in the national press invited contributions to a 'Sailors and Soldiers Christmas Fund' created by the princess, with the aim of presenting a 'gift from the nation' to 'every Sailor afloat and every Soldier at the front' on Christmas Day. The impressive sum of £162,591 12s 5d was quickly raised, and eligibility for the gift was widened to take in everyone 'wearing

The 17-year-old Princess Mary. The caption to this portrait of her in *The Illustrated War News* in early November 1914 described her as 'the royal Santa Claus', though it was the public that financed the bulk of the fund for her Christmas gift. (*The Illustrated War News*, 4 November 1914)

the King's uniform on Christmas Day, 1914', and then the wounded on leave or in hospital, nurses and the widows or parents of the fallen. Prisoners of war had theirs reserved until they came home, and while most had received their gift by the summer of 1916, even in early 1919 'considerable numbers' had reportedly still to be distributed. When the fund closed in 1920, more than 2.5 million boxes and their contents had gone out. Around 400,000 – exact estimates vary – had reached their destination by that first Christmas Day of the war.

As the order list for the boxes grew, so their quality declined. The brass came from the United States, but a large consignment went down with the *Lusitania* in May 1915 and besides, weapons and munitions, not to mention medals and memorial plaques, were ahead of pretty little tins in the pecking order for brass. The later ones came in various plated base metals and alloys, which explains why those found today vary considerably in quality. The ones made in pure brass have at least a chance of having found their way to the trenches.

The size of a typical tobacco tin of the day – 5 inches long, 3 wide, 1 deep – the boxes were designed by the studio of Messrs Adshead and Ramsey, architects who were well in with the royal family at that time. The previous year they had designed classical-influenced brick cottages for the Prince of Wales's Duchy of Cornwall estate in Courtenay Street, Lambeth, and it must have struck some palace mandarin that they were the ones to come up with a seemly, stately design for the princess's gift. And so they did, in a manner of speaking. They would have loved it in Napoleon's Empire days; but the design craze of the day was Art Nouveau in its later form, and that would surely have pleased the public at least as much. It would certainly be more to the taste of the large number of traders who are trying to offload them in quantity on the Internet today.

At the centre of the lid is a profile of Princess Mary within a laurel wreath, her initial 'M' prominent on either side. At the top in a decorative cartouche are the words 'Imperium Britannicum' with a sword and

Princess Mary's gift, a brass tobacco box of somewhat self-important but undeniably impressive design.
(*The Illustrated War Weekly*, 16 December 1914)

scabbard either side, at the bottom 'Christmas 1914', flanked by battleship bows forging through the foam. Roundels in the corner display the names of the lesser Allies, Belgium, Japan, Montenegro and Servia (*sic*), while France and Russia take pride of place along the edges, with a due flurry of flags. In a heavy-handed way – even the brass tin of chocolates sent out by Queen Victoria to the Boer War troops in 1899 was not so resolutely imperial – the little box certainly had the presence to prompt anyone who received it to keep it as a souvenir, if they had the option. Tobacco tins were handy standbys for keeping bits and pieces in, but if possible, this was definitely something for 'Keeping Nice'. Nearly forty years on, there was a commercial parallel when Oxo issued a neat little tin to commemorate the Queen's coronation in 1953; these, too, were put away by their tens of thousands after their contents had been consumed, and large numbers of them can still be found in sparkling condition.

Distributing these gifts must have been a logistical nightmare, given the conditions at the front and at sea. In fact even that first Christmas, when the gesture was still fresh, officers in charge of supplies grumbled that they were getting in the way of issuing normal rations. The standard gift, accompanied by a greetings card and a photograph of the princess, was a pipe, a tinder lighter, an ounce of tobacco and twenty cigarettes in yellow monogrammed wrappers, while non-smokers and boys were given a bullet pencil and a packet of sweets, Indians might have received sweets and spices, and there were chocolates for the nurses. Contents could vary from this, depending on supplies. Acid tablets and writing paper were among the less exciting offerings, while the most durable and collectable today was the sterling silver bullet pencil in a monogrammed brass .303 cartridge case.

As often as not these items were sent out separately from the tins themselves, which conjures up an image of some hapless orderlies in the field post offices, the whizz-bangs exploding above them, trying to make sense of the piles of tins, tobacco and confectionery all around: 'Now Captain Smith, he's a smoker, isn't he? Private Jones, don't think he likes a fag, but maybe he'll take to the pipe? Poor old Bill Brown; didn't he cop it yesterday?' This, of course, was after the tins had made their hazardous journey from Britain without being raided for their tobacco. 'Elaborate precautions were taken to prevent any loss en route to the front of the presents of the Princess Mary's Fund,' *The London Illustrated Weekly*'s *War Pictures Weekly* noted early in the New Year. 'They were conveyed in closed vans locked by letter-locks, of which the key-word was known only to certain officers. Some of the vans were also tied up with barbed wire. This great precaution nearly led to disaster in one case. The receiving officer had either forgotten or not received the opening word, "Noel", and could not get the van open until he hauled on the fastening with a motor-lorry.' On balance, it is no surprise that the grand gesture was never repeated.

The distributors' lot was not made any happier by the Christmas gifts that flooded to the front from other sources – friends and family, of course, but also from charities and the corporate hampers sent out en masse to specified recipients. The Leicester County Club sent a box of chocolates to every man in the Leicestershire Regiment – 'very nice, neat little boxes', according to one of the officers, perhaps sending out the coded message 'Do bigger next year'. On the other hand, 'Of course, the men were absolutely overcome; they were just like children at a prize distribution, and went round comparing their boxes, and making complimentary remarks about the "nibs [toffs] what sent them".'

Considerably more generously, although targeting fewer numbers, the directors and workers at a brewery in Guildford had a whip-round and sent to each of their colleagues at the front a Christmas hamper that deserves to be celebrated in detail: 2-pound Christmas pudding; tin of tongue; two tins sardines; tin Irish stew; two chickens; two tins bloater paste; large packet chocolate; Oxo; large tin biscuits; tin salmon; tin pineapple; mustard, salt, pepper; tin opener; peppermints; paper and pencil; soap; two packs of playing cards. A handsome gift by anybody's standards, although one worries rather about the fate of the chickens. 'There's all the stuff

in the newspapers about Tommy at the Front enjoying a full Christmas dinner, and all we got was cold
bully beef and cold pudding,' one of the lads not
lucky enough to be a brewery worker in Guildford
complained; shades of the glistening plastic turkey
borne in triumph into the Iraq mess room by George
W. Bush in December 2003 before his troops were
given 'airline-style meals of pre-packaged meat'.

Then there were all the commercial organisations
with their various promotions – free Christmas puddings from the *Daily Mail*, chocolate from Cadbury's,
butterscotch toffee from Callard & Bowser, Wills'
cut-price cigarette offers. Friends and relatives could
send 1,000 Woodbines to their man at the front for
9 shillings, 1,000 Gold Flakes for 15 shillings, both
complete with a cheery Christmas card. Given the
limited resources open to them, compared to today,
the marketing men of a century ago were up to all the
tricks. 'I am keeping well in spite of the large number
of Christmas parcels received,' a rifleman wrote home
on Christmas Eve, displaying a fine taste in twenty-
first century irony.

Princess Mary, born in 1897, gained a higher public
profile as the war went on, coming of age just a few
months before it ended. She regularly visited hospitals
and welfare organisations, actively promoting the Girl
Guide movement, the Voluntary Aid Detachment and
the Women's Land Army. In 1918 she took a nursing course and went to work at Great Ormond Street,

and retained her interest in the Guides, the women's services and nursing up to her comparatively early death in 1965. Her marriage to the considerably older Viscount Lascelles, who became Earl of Harewood, was said to have been forced on her by her parents; one story doing the rounds was that he had proposed to her to win a bet at his club. That said, they seemed a contented enough couple to those who knew them as the years passed by.

Her loyalty to her brother David after his abdication as Edward VIII also allegedly put her at odds with the royal establishment, despite her being granted the title Princess Royal in 1932. She and her husband went to stay with David (by now the Duke of Windsor) at Enzenfeld Castle, near Vienna, and in 1947 she is said to have turned down an invitation to Princess Elizabeth's wedding, pleading ill health, in protest against the palace's decision not to invite the Windsors. At the outbreak of the Second World War she became chief controller and then controller commandant of the Auxiliary Territorial Service, and other duties and honours followed. Away from her official life, however, it is the 1939–45 war that created one of the nation's most abiding collective memories of her; whether or not it is a false memory remains open to doubt.

It was in Harrods that the famously forgetful Sir Thomas Beecham encountered a pleasant-looking woman in her early middle years, and knew he had met her somewhere.

'Hello, Madam. And how are you?'

'I'm very well, thank you, but I do worry about my brother. He's working far too hard.'

'Ah yes, your brother. And what's he doing these days.'

'Oh, he's still King.'

Many variations of this story have proliferated since then, but it does not seem to have surfaced much before it appeared in a biography of Sir Thomas published in 1943. You never know, it could even be true.

# BRAVE HEARTS
## TO THE FRONT

It was a spectacle as extraordinary as any ever seen
on a British football ground. On cold winter after-
noons in Edinburgh, half-time was usually reserved
for hot pies and Bovril and hanging around the
refreshment hut for as long as possible to soak up any
warmth that might come your way; but on Saturday,
5 December 1914, hordes of local men had something
very different in mind. They poured on to the pitch
to enlist for the army, or, more precisely, McCrae's
Own Battalion. The game was a local derby at Heart
of Midlothian's Tynecastle ground against their old
foe Hibernian, and hundreds of 'Jam Tarts' fans were
joined by scores of 'Hibees' in showing loyalty to
their country.

The man who inspired them, whatever their political or sporting persuasion, was Lieutenant Colonel
Sir George McCrae, a prominent magistrate, local
politician and businessman, a textile merchant by
trade, who had served as a Liberal MP for Edinburgh

East for ten years until 1909 and was proud to be an army volunteer. He made no pretence about his background – the illegitimate son of a housemaid, who never knew his father – and was admired all the more for that. He also had a way with words, and in the previous month, before the introduction of conscription, he had been given permission to try to raise a battalion for the Royal Scots. Aged 54, and cutting a somewhat incongruous figure, tartan-clad on horseback, he was not everyone's idea of a battlefield leader; but he gave the men plenty to think about, the Hearts-Hibs game turned into the glorious climax to his recruitment drive, and so the Royal Scots' Sixteenth Battalion, McCrae's Own, came into being.

Even before that day, thirteen Hearts players had answered the call to arms, and more soon followed; seven of them were to go on and die in battle. At the time they were top of the Scottish League, having won their first eight games, and looked set fair for their first championship since 1897; but among sportsmen they were very quick to see that whatever their fellow countryman Bill Shankly might have had to say years later, there are rather more important things in life than football.

In truth, plenty of people were keen to remind them of this fact, with young men dying by their thousands out in France while these fine specimens of manhood continued to be paid to kick a bag of wind around the field as though everything was normal.

Nevertheless, the pressure was on every team alike in
Scotland – and to their lasting credit, it was Hearts
who were first to rise magnificently to the call. Others
who followed them into the battalion were professionals from Raith Rovers, Falkirk and Dunfermline, along
with men from some seventy-five local Edinburgh-area
clubs, rugby and hockey players, strongmen, golfers,
bowlers and field athletes.

In his appeal to the crowd, McCrae was able to
point to these fine fellows as true examples to follow,
and there is no doubt that their involvement was
crucial to his cause. Up and down the country, Pals'
battalions, made up of men from the same communities, factories, sports leagues or interest groups,
had become a key component in the recruiting campaign. The Royal Scots' Sixteenth, the Edinburgh
footballers' and fans' battalion, was quickly seen as
a classic example of the breed.

The tragedy of Pals' battalions, as became all
too apparent as hostilities wore on, was that if
they met with disaster, the impact on their home
communities was all the greater. So it was with
McCrae's Own. In the words of Jack Alexander,
the author of the definitive history of the battalion:

> McCrae's men crossed to France in 1916, and on July 1
> they took part in the infamous opening day of the
> Battle of the Somme. They were selected to assault the
> most dangerous part of the enemy position, a fearsome

network of barbed wire and entrenchments, bristling with machine-guns. In spite of this, they took every objective and achieved the deepest penetration of the German line anywhere on the front; in the process they lost three-quarters of their strength.

McCrae himself, by this time promoted to full colonel, was swiftly withdrawn from the front line, invalided home and returned to the ranks of reservists. As far as the top brass were concerned, the inspirational recruitment officer was out of his depth on the front line, an amateur among professionals, and on balance, their judgment was doubtless correct. His men, what was left of them, never lost their faith in him or affection for him, and his bravery was never in question; but as a proactive leader in an integrated modern army, he understandably did not quite measure up. Though he was awarded the Distinguished Service Order, this was almost routine for senior officers at that time.

The Royal Scots' Sixteenth Battalion was reconstituted later in the war, and saw brave and distinguished service at Arras in April 1917, Passchendaele later that year, and Lys in the German spring offensive of 1918, when with others it held its line in the face of a furious enemy onslaught. By this time, many of the troops in its ranks knew little or nothing of Colonel McCrae, and for those few who did, December 1914 seemed a long, long time ago.

After the war, from 1919 to 1922, McCrae served as chairman of the Scottish Board of Health before a brief return to Westminster. He failed as a Lloyd George National Liberal against the sitting Labour MP in Edinburgh Central in 1922, but squeezed in for the Liberals at Stirling and Falkirk Burghs the following year, with a majority of 156. October 1924 brought a further election after Ramsay MacDonald's minority Labour Government had lost a motion of no confidence, and while the Conservatives won by a landslide, Labour comfortably regained their seat in Sterling. It was the election that spelled the end of the Liberals as major contenders for government, and for McCrae it was the finale to a long career in the public eye. He died four years later, aged 68.

As for Hearts, they had to wait until 1958 for their next Scottish League championship. Remarkably, the league's first division continued throughout the war, and at the end of the season Celtic came out victorious with 65 points, 4 points more than the men from Tynecastle. Success in football was a gamble in those years, with player absentees, guest players and inexperienced youths filling the gaps, and constantly the demoralising drip-feed of tragic news of old friends and colleagues at the front; a lottery – but one that was won every season by either Celtic or Rangers. It takes more than a world war to upset the balance of Scottish football.

And that might have been the end of the story had it not been for Jack Alexander and his book *McCrae's Battalion* (2003). 'The research took me twelve years and involved tracing more than a thousand families of Sir George's original volunteers,' Mr Alexander revealed, continuing:

> The resultant mountain of letters, diaries, photographs and personal recollection unearthed a long-abandoned plan from 1919 for a memorial to the battalion – a fourteen-foot-high Scottish cairn in the rebuilt village of Contalmaison, complete with a large bronze-relief plaque to record McCrae's men's sacrifice for generations to come.
>
> When the book was about to appear, I was invited to a meeting at Tynecastle; after a supporter had visited the Western Front and noticed that there was no memorial to the Hearts players who had died on the Somme, a small committee had been formed, independently of the club, to explore the possibility of putting this right. They had drawn up plans for a dedicated Hearts memorial, but before my meeting with them ended they had torn them up and committed themselves instead to helping me complete the original scheme.

The cairn was unveiled by members of the McCrae's Battalion Trust in 2004, and a party has returned every year since. Mr Alexander had no record of the planned wording of the original plaque, but came up with an apt inscription. Two further plaques were added, one dedicated to the players and supporters of Hearts and the other to the Royal Scots' Fifteenth Battalion, made up of men from Edinburgh and Manchester, which fought alongside the McCrae's that morning.

It did not end there. Half a mile away from Contalmaison, the village of Pozieres holds an annual ceremony of remembrance, and in 2011 it staged an informal re-enactment of that Hearts-Hibs match of December 1914, with amateur players who then joined the spectators to recreate the mass enlistment. There was fighting in and around Pozieres for more than a month, and the first day of the Battle of the Somme, 1 July 1916, is now known as the blackest day in the history of the British Army, with some 20,000 men killed and twice that number injured. More than 250 of McCrae's band died in that first onslaught, with hundreds more injured. 'I was never prouder of my lads than on that day,' he later recalled; but as too often in the First World War, the price of undreamed-of heroism was undreamed-of bloodshed.

# THE BELGIAN
## INVASION

The Belgian refugees make up a subplot of the First
World War that attracts little attention today, but
their presence was a prominent feature of local life
in a large number of communities around Britain.
They started coming over within weeks of the
outbreak of war, and the generally warm reception
extended to them was cemented by concerted efforts
to make them feel welcome and at home at Christmas,
especially where children were concerned. Some
inevitable tensions developed as the war ground on,
and that strange first Christmas was undoubtedly the
high point of our nation's outpouring of goodwill
towards them; but this was the greatest mass-immi-
gration Britain had ever seen, and overall we can be
proud of our ancestors in the way they handled it.

It was in September 1914 that the British
Government offered 'victims of war the hospitality of
the British nation', and local committees, consisting of
the usual kind of people who form local committees,

Remember Belgium, a propaganda poster that served the dual purpose of engendering hatred towards the Germans and warning Britons of what would be in store if the foe reached these shores. (LC-USZC4-10881)

sprang up to put this sentiment into action. It was Germany's invasion of Belgium, after all, that by terms of treaty had drawn Britain into the war, and the authorities felt no compunction to quell a flood of lurid stories of atrocities towards women and children: the 'Remember Belgium' poster campaign, with its poignant image of innocents turned out of their homes into a desperately uncertain future, was calculated not only to stiffen British resistance to invasion but to engage with neutral countries.

There was also a strong feeling that 'Brave Little Belgium' did not deserve to suffer the hapless fate of falling victim to circumstances beyond its control. Writing in the *Stroud News* on December 18, the spokesman for the Painswick refugee committee observed that: 'The duty of relieving these homeless wanderers is not merely the charity due to their misfortunes; it is a payment of a debt that can never be discharged to the people who have been made the scapegoat for the sins of Europe.' The measured tone of that last phrase, it must be said, did not chime in with the anti-German hysteria raging in the bulk of the British press.

The horror stories prompted Prime Minister Herbert Asquith to call on James, Viscount Bryce, a barrister and former ambassador to Washington, to head a 'Committee on Alleged German Outrages', and when it reported in May 1915 it is clear that it had taken many uncorroborated accounts at face

The cruel, arrogant Germans in Belgium as seen by a
*Penny War Weekly* cartoonist. The young woman is having
a rosette in her country's national colours snatched
off her – a mild indignity, compared with the horrors
many propagandists were hinting at. (*Penny War Weekly*,
19 September 1914)

value, including those supplied by refugees. Again, America took note of what it heard, but over the years, many of the report's more sensational stories were discredited. On the other hand, invading armies have never been noted for their good manners towards women, to put it mildly, while the Germans in Belgium (frustrated that their Schlieffen Plan to capture Paris was apparently being thwarted by saboteurs and guerrillas) dealt harshly with any suspects they captured, along with the communities they believed were harbouring them.

As well as destroying historic and significant buildings and fouling households' food, they executed some 6,000 French and Belgian civilians between August and November 1914, usually in shootings ordered at random by officers on the spot. Researchers have traced German Army records of 101 'major' incidents in which ten or more civilians were killed, totalling 4,421 deaths, along with 383 'minor' incidents in which a further 1,100 died. Almost all were claimed to be in response to widespread 'illegal' activities which deserved immediate collective punishment, though it is now accepted that, understandably, there was little or no organised resistance in those first few frantic months. In other words, while the Germans overreacted grotesquely to perceived opposition, tales of decapitated children and babies hanging from bayonets had little or no basis in reality.

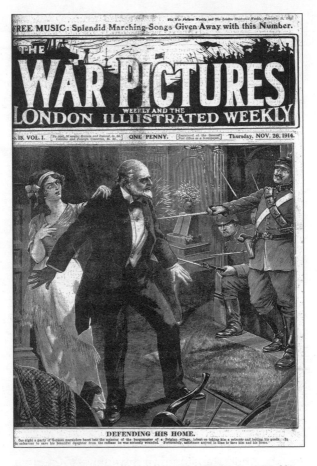

FREE MUSIC: Splendid Marching-Songs Given Away with this Number.

# THE WAR PICTURES
### WEEKLY AND THE
## LONDON ILLUSTRATED WEEKLY

No. 15, VOL. I. | ONE PENNY. | Thursday, NOV. 26, 1914.

**DEFENDING HIS HOME.**

One night a party of German marauders burst into the mansion of the burgomaster of a Belgian village, intent on taking him a prisoner and looting his goods. In his endeavour to save his beautiful daughter from the ruffians he was seriously wounded. Fortunately, assistance arrived in time to save him and his home.

Here they come again, this time in *The War Pictures Weekly*: a Belgian burgomaster defends his beautiful daughter, but 'fortunately, assistance arrived in time to save him and his home'. The feisty looking daughter was presumably well able to take care of herself. (*The War Pictures Weekly*)

Belgium had a population of 7.5 million in 1914, and maybe 1.5 million of them fled. Most settled in the Netherlands but an estimated 250,000 found their way to Britain. Inevitably, life was at least as hard for those who stayed at home, and the focus of food and aid from several neutral countries, notably the United States, was on them. There would doubtless have been a humanitarian disaster if it had not been provided, and extensive and largely successful efforts were made to ensure that provisions did not fall into enemy hands. Britain, on the other hand, was reluctant to support the project, insisting that Germany should be held responsible for feeding its occupied territories, and Winston Churchill saw the relief effort as 'a positive military disaster'.

In terms of numbers the Belgian refugees were very much on a par with the Jews in Britain; but while the latter tended to be concentrated in major cities, notably London, Manchester, Leeds and Glasgow, the Belgians were everywhere, welcomed and nurtured in communities in a way that later, when the novelty had worn off, had some cynics muttering about 'spoiled pets'. It is clear that an underlying factor in the initial positive reaction was the understanding that it would 'all be over by Christmas', and families who had at first welcomed these strangers into their homes were forced to admit it would be best for all concerned for them to live independently. Employment for the men emerged as

A French artist's version of the miseries of life with the
invaders, even when they were not being physically violent:
a drunk German officer sprawls over the family's best and
possibly only bed. (*The Illustrated War News*, 4 November 1914)

a major concern; a strong contingent went to work
on the railways, others joined either their own or
the British Army, and munitions factories at Birtley,
County Durham and Richmond, Surrey were such
major employers that refugee 'villages' grew up
beside them, with their own Belgian police force;
the Birtley one was given the name Elisabethville,
in honour of the Queen of the Belgians, and it is
known as that to this day.

In other parts of the country groups of specialist
workers were encouraged to go back to their own
trades or crafts. In Painswick, Gloucestershire, for

instance, where the five-dozen refugees were from the French-speaking Malines, men who included a sawyer, woodcarver, carpenters, cabinetmakers and chair-makers were helped to set up a business making chairs in a disused factory, managed by a committee of local people and one of their own. 'No wages are paid, the workers and their families being maintained by this committee, but any profits will be for the benefit of the Belgians concerned,' the *Stroud News* reported. By and large, trade unions, weakened as they were by war, seem to have been tolerant of such ventures.

Belgian refugee children arriving in London in the early days of the war, in an excellent photograph from the *Great Deeds Of The Great War* weekly. What a steep learning curve lay ahead for these youngsters and those looking after them. (*T.P.'s Journal Of Great Deeds Of The Great War*, 31 October 1914)

The *Stroud News*'s editions around Christmas 1914
and the New Year were full of accounts of goodwill
towards the Belgians. At the local Empire's festive
show, 'Little Miss Page, who sings very sweetly a
charming little child's song, "Daddy's Gone To
The War", appears at each house in aid of the Belgian
refugees. She has been very popular, and the chorus
of her song is enthusiastically taken up by her hear-
ers, while her collecting box has been readily filled.'
On Boxing Day, Stroud Rugby Club was able to muster
a fifteen to hammer the locally based company of the
Army Service Corps in the name of charity towards
the refugees, while 'in the different homes where they
were being taken care of, everything was done to make
the season as bright and happy as possible'.

The culmination of the charm offensive came
on New Year's Eve, when 'by the kindness of
Lady Marling, a Christmas entertainment for the
Belgians now staying in the district was given in the
Subscription Rooms'. Some 200 of them gathered in
the big hall which was:

> Decorated on an extensive scale ... A platform had been
> erected opposite to the balcony, tastefully arranged with a
> quantity of fine plants, flowers and evergreens, while on
> one side was a gorgeous Christmas tree decorated with all
> manner of fancy articles and fairy candles. The windows
> were draped with red and white bunting, while two lines
> of gaily coloured flags were suspended from the four

corners of the hall. On the massive mantelshelf were
draped the Belgian colours, while at the other end of the
room hung a large union jack ... French, Russian and
more British flags were suspended on every wall, and evergreens and plants arranged on the front of the balcony
and mantelshelf lent a refreshing effect to the scene.

Tea was served on two tables running the length of
the room, 'waited on by a host of helpers who were
daintily attired in white dresses, with caps and aprons
in the popular red, orange and black. The prevailing
theme of compliment to the Belgian nation was a
great source of delight to the appreciative guests.'
For entertainment there followed:

A conjuror employed by Lady Marling and a programme
of largely light classical music by Miss Eltringham and
other young ladies.

Father Stephen Fitzgerald, the local Roman Catholic
priest who had done much to make the Belgians feel
welcome over the previous months, sang 'Ave Maria' followed by Charles Kingsley's tragic parlour song 'Three
Fishers', the one in which 'Men must work, and women
must weep, And there's little to earn, and many to keep,
Though the harbour bar be moaning'.

Not typical festive fare, perhaps, but thankfully, Miss
Marguerite Godfrey 'completely charmed the audience
with a couple of happy little songs, "Agatha Green"

and "Catch Me!", for which she was heartily applauded, while Miss Eltringham gave a delightful song, "What's In The Air Today", which was received with enthusiasm. A little Belgian girl sang the National Anthem, for which she was encored, her country people heartily taking up the refrain.'

Time was passing by too quickly, but:

> Later in the evening the lights were lowered and the beautiful Christmas tree was illuminated, the brilliant spectacle being received with rapturous cheering on the part of the little ones. Each child had a pretty gift, formally presented by Mrs Allen and Mr M.G. Cartwright.

After that, it remained only for the hall to be cleared for dancing, 'the music being provided by the band, and then after a beautiful supper had been done full justice to, the Belgians were taken back to their homes'. That was Christmas for the refugees in one small English town, and it was a scene repeated the length and breadth of the land. Neither should we suppose that all the Lady Marlings, Mrs Allens and Mr Cartwrights, not to mention every last helper slavishly noted by the press, were motivated by anything other than the goodness of their hearts. The newspapers printed their names simply because that is what local newspapers did.

We have reflected that the refugees were never again fawned over in quite the way they were that first

Christmas, but then again, they progressed in other ways. They found work, and before long their children were helping them along with their English, as often as not complete with their neighbours' local accent. Oddly, though not uniquely, it was cosmopolitan London that had the most trouble coping with them, and the depressing mantra of 'over here taking our jobs and our houses', still so familiar today, led to anti-Belgian unrest in May 1916. By nothing more than coincidence it was a clergyman's daughter from near Stroud, scene of the festivities noted above, who later dismissed the refugees as 'fat, lazy, greedy, amiable and inclined to take all the benefits heaped on them as a matter of course', while 'Belgian atrocity' was such a press cliché that it became easy to apply it to the refugee kid who pinched an apple off your tree or rude workman who barged in front of you in the bus queue. Then again, an elderly Belgian woman was heard to complain that the British were unbelievably lazy, because they relied on men in traps to deliver their milk and boys on bicycles their meat, bread and groceries.

It was a learning curve for both sides, and it is not surprising that at the end of the war most of the Belgians elected to go back home. Maybe 20,000 stayed on, most of them in towns where there was industrial work and the chance to pick up the language quickly and feel part of a tight-knit community with its pubs, football and churches. And then, according to

Agatha Christie, there was one Hercule Poirot, whom she introduced in *The Mysterious Affair At Styles*, published in 1920 but written in 1916, and who made his final departure, in print at least, in *Curtain* in 1975. It was as a refugee that the former pride of the Brussels police force, apparently brought up near Spa, found himself solving crimes in English country houses.

In 1930 Agatha Christie confessed that she was finding Poirot 'insufferable', and by 1960 he was a 'detestable, bombastic, tiresome, egocentric little creep', invective that even a vicar's daughter from Stroud would have been hard-pressed to emulate when describing a Belgian refugee. Yet the writer knew that while her fans loved him, she must stay with M. Poirot; he was a Belgian who was not easy to forget, and up and down the country there are scattered families who, because of friendships forged 100 years ago, still exchange Christmas cards with increasingly distant and mysterious households on the other side of the Channel.

# THE FIRST
# SUBMARINER VC

The Allies' battle with the Ottoman Turks in the Dardanelles Straits in 1915 was a military disaster, with action around their northern shores adding the name of Gallipoli to the likes of Ypres, the Somme and Passchendaele in Britain's chronicle of the war's darkest hours. Yet it all began, in the days before Christmas 1914, in a way that gave the press every opportunity to wave the flag – and earned the first Victoria Cross in that theatre of war. What is more, the recipient lived to tell the tale and be honoured in a further extraordinary way – and that could not be said of many Dardanelles VCs.

It was on 13 December when the submarine B11 shattered the comparative calm of the western mouth of the straits by diving under five rows of mines in treacherous currents to torpedo and sink the Turkish battleship *Mesudiye*, which had been posted to guard the minefield. The sub's 26-year-old commander, Lieutenant Norman Douglas Holbrook,

then succeeded in returning his vessel to the
Mediterranean by running the gauntlet of shore
batteries and torpedo boats in a mission that had
seen her submerged for some nine hours. That
was hailed as a staggering feat in itself at that time,
and Holbrook was duly feted for it. His was the first
VC to be awarded to a submariner, and the first to be
awarded to any naval officer in this war.

It came at a time when the eastern Mediterranean
was not seen as a priority by the War Office, and the
press made much of the fact that the B11 was
at best obsolescent, nine years old at a time when
technology by land, sea and air was advancing at a
bewildering pace. What was less well publicised was
the fact that the British-built *Mesudiye* – officially

Intrepid feat: the sinking of the *Mesudiye* by Norman
Holbrook's B11 submarine, as envisaged by a *War Pictures
Weekly* artist. (*War Pictures Weekly*, 31 December 1914)

'the Royal Armoured Frigate *Mesudiye*' – was even older, first commissioned as an Ironclad in 1875 and rebuilt in a pre-Dreadnought style in 1903. She had recently seen lively active service against the Greeks in the First Balkan War in late 1912 and early 1913, and her captain and senior officers were deeply unimpressed by her passive new role as an anchored protector of the minefield just south of the Dardanelles Narrows in Sarisiglar Bay.

The blow from the B11 came at precisely noon on 13 December, when she released a torpedo from a range of 800 metres. Lookouts on the ship saw the submarine's disappearing periscope and indeed the oncoming torpedo before it struck, but there was precious little time to retaliate, and the fact that most of the crew were below decks eating lunch contributed to the B11's escape. The *Mesudiye* capsized in ten minutes, trapping most of the crew; thirty-seven of them died, but the water was so shallow that most were saved by rescuers cutting through the hull. The ship's guns were also recovered and mounted in a shore battery that was given her name; three months later, on 18 March 1915, they were blazing again to strike the French battleship *Bouvet* eight times. They failed to deliver a knockout blow, but the mines they were defending accounted for her, and sank her within two minutes, leading to the death of well over 600 men. The British in the same raiding party took the explosion to have been caused by a shell or torpedo and steamed on into the minefield, where the pre-Dreadnoughts *Ocean* and *Irresistible* were sunk and the battle cruiser *Inflexible* was badly damaged, again with distressing loss of life.

A disastrous day, then, and one that put the B11's audacious but only partially effective pre-Christmas heroics into perspective. It was also a major factor in the decision to abandon a naval attack on Constantinople, and instead opt for a land campaign focusing on Gallipoli. A considerable disaster that led to a catastrophic disaster: it was an early example of an alarming pattern which became all too familiar to both sides in the war as their policies lurched from one crisis to another.

As for Norman Holbrook, who ended his naval career as a commander, his Victoria Cross led to the Australian town of Germanton, New South Wales, changing its name in his honour to Holbrook in August 1915. Deeply touched by the gesture, he struck up a close relationship with the community as the years passed by, visiting it three times in his lifetime from his home in Sussex. He died in 1976, aged 87, but his widow kept up the link with passion, presenting his VC medal to this landlocked community in 1982 and making a substantial donation towards a submariners' memorial, a striking piece of work in the form of a scale model of the B11, in 1995. Two years later she visited Holbrook to unveil it, while since then a bronze statue of her husband has been put up in the town's Germanton Park. His medal group, including the Victoria Cross, was loaned to the Australian War Memorial in 2009 and is on display there, while a replica can be seen at Holbrook's submarine museum.

A remarkable story: it was merely the coincidence of topicality that led this far-off community to name itself after him. A few months either way, and Holbrook today would go under an entirely different name; but it chose this brave, resourceful man on whom to bestow this singular honour, and one who could not have entered more into the spirit of the gesture.

# KNITTING
# FOR VICTORY

Lord Kitchener's stern gaze from the recruiting posters is credited with calling hundreds of thousands of young men to the nation's cause, but he was equally adept at mobilising women to the war effort. On 3 October 1914 the *Penny War Weekly* reported that:

> In view of the special winter requirements, and to supplement the provision made by the War Office, Lord Kitchener has asked the Queen to supply 300,000 belts, knitted or woven, and 300,000 pairs of socks, to be ready, if possible, early in November. Lord Kitchener has kindly promised that these articles shall be immediately distributed at the front. The Queen has willingly acceded to the request and asks the women of the Empire to assist her in making this offering to the troops.

In truth, some women's groups were already well under way by then, and notional requirements in their hundreds of thousands soon went out of the window.

By the end of 1918 the War Office had issued some 137,225,000 pairs of socks over the course of hostilities, and while the hosiers of Leicester and elsewhere had profited mightily from this, the part played by home-knitters was significant; besides, what the above vast figure ignores is the additional contribution of all sorts of garments in morale-boosting gifts and comforts packets.

Kitchener, by no means averse to publicity, even put his name to a knitting stitch still recognised today, as well as a sock with a seamless toe. Whoever designed it, the Secretary of State for War would have taken a keen interest in it, since well-meant but uncomfortable foot-wear could be the source of real trouble in the trenches. Women suddenly found that making a pair of bootees for their new grandchild or a school sweater for their son or daughter was tantamount to 'Knitting for the Kaiser', no less. Success in the war was a universal struggle, and by knitting for victory they could play as vital a part in that struggle as the boys at the front. 'The First World War stimulated British knitting to the point where it was regarded as a national mania,' Richard Rutt noted in his book *A History Of Hand Knitting*.

The Red Cross was swiftly off the mark, organising work parties to sew and knit garments for wounded servicemen. Like Kitchener, the organisation recognised the need for uniformity, and put out large numbers of instruction booklets with patterns for pyjamas, socks, dressing gowns and so on. Keen committee women rose to the challenge with relish, setting up not only regular meetings of helpers but extensive networks of knitters and needlewomen who preferred to work at home. The working party of women in the villages of Bisley and Eastcombe, near Stroud, for instance, met on Wednesdays at the Court House in Bisley but also distributed material for other women in the area to work on. 'The population of our parish may be small, but that cannot be said of the patriotism of our people,' the group's spokeswoman, Mrs Bloodworth, told the local paper. 'Our Roll of Honour numbers more than eighty, and the ladies have shown themselves as patriotic as our brave men.' Nearly 250 villagers had subscribed some £26 towards the cost of materials, and the cloth-ing had gone out to regional committees collecting for the Belgian refugees, the Red Cross, hospital ships and for men in France and in the navy, with the stipulation that these packages should go to local men.

Twenty-four Christmas packages were put together for Bisley and Eastcombe soldiers and sailors, consisting of what now seems a rather uninspired set of offerings: a flannel shirt, three pairs of socks, a handkerchief, and for the sailors, an additional pair of mittens. The ladies seemed much more engaged when it came to making clothes for women and children, deluging the local branch of the Women's International Relief Committee for Belgian Refugees with all manner of dresses, jerseys, skirts, petticoats, blouses, underwear, 'little socks' and 'little vests'. They also donated hospital goods to the Red Cross, while girls at Bisley School turned the focus back on the fighting men, making seventy items including woollen body belts, socks, mittens, caps, scarves and handkerchiefs in their spare time. The Bisley women were certainly on the ball with their extra mittens for sailors. One of the most popular patterns published came with the approval of the Royal National Mission to Deep Sea Fishermen, a reminder that it was the trawlermen who were at the forefront of Britain's minesweeping operation.

It was the age range of women doing their bit for the country that fascinated the press, especially as Christmas approached. Schoolgirls were much in evidence in photographs, busy with their knitting needles, as was everybody from chorus girls in their West End dressing rooms to munitions workers on their lunch break. 'Mrs Conybeare of Clydach holds that no woman is too old to help her country,' was the caption to a picture of what looked to be an extremely old lady in the *Penny War Weekly*. 'In early girlhood she knitted for our soldiers in the Crimea. When she was passing her prime she was making articles of clothing for our troops in South Africa. Now, at the age of seventy-eight, the dear old Welsh lady is making shirts and socks for our fighting men in France.'

Nowhere in the country were the women better organised than in Tamworth, Staffordshire, where on 31 August 1914, the local Women's Liberal Association was disbanded, to be replaced by the Tamworth Ladies'

Working League. 'We, the members of the Women's Liberal Association, in view of the immediate and urgent need for practical effort on the part of all women in this hour of national peril, pledge ourselves to assist in every way in alleviating the sorrow and suffering which must come to our land through the war, and irrespective of political party, religious creeds or social distinctions, unite ourselves in working for our soldiers and for the common good of all,' their statement read.

The league was launched with a loan of £1 10s from the kitty of the old club, and soon the whole town was rallying round with donations in cash and kind, not least knitting wool for socks. By the time Lord Kitchener was making his first appeal, the women of Tamworth were already up and at it. Meeting every Monday at the Co-op's Baths and Institute in Church Street, by Christmas Day they were able to send a hamper of socks, mufflers and fifty pairs of pants to the Tamworth Territorials preparing for duty at a camp in Saffron Walden, along with tobacco and plum puddings. Their captain wrote a gracious letter of thanks; apparently the lads had enjoyed their Christmas, and the plum puddings had gone down very well with their festive meal.

The Tamworth league remained high-profile and active locally throughout the war, promoting an imaginative programme of fundraisers and relief efforts; and two Christmases on, in December 1916, it launched a venture that made the town's railway station famous far and wide, wherever servicemen

As well as knitwear, Christmas puddings were another favourite gift for soldiers and sailors at the sharp end. Few, however, could have been as splendid as this one being enjoyed by Tommy and his gallant allies on the cover of *War Pictures Weekly*'s Christmas Eve number. (*War Pictures Weekly*, 24 December 1914)

gathered to reminisce about warm welcomes and good grub. Tamworth was at the junction of two main lines, and it had become disturbing to see soldiers and sailors milling around the platforms waiting for their connections, often cold and hungry. The women's idea was to set up a buffet, the stationmaster said yes, and the local gas company paid to convert part of a waiting room into a kitchen, complete with stove and boiler. The food was unlike anything anywhere else on the main lines for tastiness, and there were even blankets, rugs and cushions to help ease long waits. The service continued until March 1919, when the last of the homecoming troops passed through the station.

As for the Tamworth Territorials, they left Saffron Walden for France in late February 1915, but spent the following Christmas in Egypt before arriving back in Europe at Marseilles in February, 1916. Around 100 of them were plunged into the Battle of the Somme, but twenty-eight of them never returned home and forty-two others were wounded, a merciless casualty rate. The ladies' comforts hamper of Christmas 1914, the woolly mufflers and plum duffs, must have seemed a long time ago.

Trench foot, of course was the big fear, and it could set in quickly. Standing in damp conditions of less than 16°C for as little as half a day could trigger it, especially in tight footwear. Feet would turn red or blue and swell due to poor blood supply; as cells started to die, ulcers and finally gangrene would set in, and the amputation of a toe or limb was common. An added stress for the Tommies was that their commanding officers were increasingly inclined to put the burden of preventing trench foot on them, presenting their failure to keep their feet warm and dry as a self-inflicted wound, on a par with being laid low with sunburn. By 1915 they were issued with three pairs of socks and were under orders to change them twice a day, but quite how this was going to work day-in, day-out when lives were lived in ankle-deep mud was a mystery to the troops – not to mention their junior officers and NCOs, whose responsibility it was to ensure that their men took all appropriate measures to look after their feet.

All too often, 'appropriate' could only be interpreted as 'as well as could be hoped for in the circumstances'; duckboards at the foot of the trenches helped a little, and there might be a few sets of thigh-length rubber waders around for the lucky ones. Otherwise, it was a case of anything that might help the cause: scarfs, bits of newspaper, empty sandbags. Standard-issue puttees were just about the last thing needed, wrapped tight round the calf and restricting the blood supply. By 1916, those millions of women still knitting so assiduously would have been horrified to see the men daubing whale oil all over their feet and dispensing with socks altogether; but at Christmas 1914, with Lord Kitchener's earnest appeal ringing in their ears, they could not have been more convinced that they were answering their country's call.

# A POET IS BORN

Edward Thomas is best known today as a poet, famous for one special piece of verse but the writer of 150 or so others, all of them still in print. The one we know best is 'Adlestrop', that outlandish station name on the Great Western Railway's line from Paddington to Worcester that caught his eye when his train stopped there in June 1914, and prompted him later to immortalise it in a haunting elegy for a long-lost world of rural fastness and endless birdsong.

It was six months after that, in the days leading up to Christmas 1914, that he turned his thoughts towards writing poetry. Up until then he had been a busy literary journeyman and journalist, adept at reviewing books – he could happily leaf through a dozen or more a week – turning out biographies and writing about the countryside. In 1913 he had even produced a novel, *The Happy-Go-Lucky Morgans*, but it had hardly changed his life.

And then, suddenly, this great outpouring of poetry. Where did it come from? The literal answer was that most of it came from deep inside him, though the more practical explanation was that it had been inspired and encouraged by the group of poets who had all too briefly gathered in and around the village of Dymock, in the north-western corner of Gloucestershire that rolled away into Herefordshire. Its resident mainstays were the so-called 'Georgian' poets Lascelles Abercrombie and Wilfrid Gibson, but the American Robert Frost was also renting a house there, and visitors included Rupert Brooke, the dramatist John Drinkwater and Thomas, whose (probably platonic) companion Eleanor Farjeon was often not far away.

Abercrombie, Brooke, Drinkwater and Gibson, who knew of one another through contributing to the *Westminster Gazette*, were figures at the heart of the Georgian movement. As George V had come to the throne only in 1910 they saw themselves and were seen as pace-setters, favouring a simple, direct style and down-to-earth themes; it was their misfortune to be at a stage in social history in which the world would be turned on its head, and in literary history where the revolutionary likes of T.S. Eliot and Ezra Pound were lurking in the wings.

Abercrombie, today regarded as a decidedly lesser poet, was in many ways the central figure in the Dymock circle, and he felt warmly towards Thomas as a critic who had written enthusiastically about his first two books of verse, in 1908 and 1911; more recently, in the *New Weekly* and *Daily Chronicle* in February 1914, Thomas had heaped praise on the first issue of *New Numbers*, an occasional journal produced by Gibson and Abercrombie and containing new poems by both of them as well as Drinkwater and Brooke. Thomas was living not an impossible way away from Dymock, at Steep in Hampshire, and he soon learned to enjoy the company there.

The New Englander Robert Frost was a particular favourite of his; he felt they had an affinity and was intrigued when Frost began to encourage him to write poetry as a result of reading his new book *In Pursuit of Spring*, which traced in lyrical prose Thomas's cycling and walking tour from Clapham Common to the Quantock Hills in Somerset. A month later, in May 1914, Frost won almost instant literary celebrity with his collection *North of Boston*, still seen by many to be his best book of poetry. For a figure of this stature to be urging him to write poems was quite a fillip for the habitually downtrodden Thomas, and though widely seen to be unhappily married, he planned to move to Dymock for a month with his wife Helen and children to be near Frost. His chosen date for the move was August 1914 ...

That did not happen, but his conversion to writing poetry did, and it was in the last days of 1914 that the floodgates opened. 'My works come pouring in on you now,' he wrote to Frost on 15 December, less than two weeks after completing his first poem. 'Tell me all you dare about them.' On the same day he wrote to his old contact Harold Monro at the Poetry Bookshop in London, sending him a sheaf of manuscripts and declaring that he 'would like to see a book of these and others'. Used to instant prose and instant payment, however modest the latter might have been, he had neither the inclination nor the means to see his poems sitting around doing nothing for any length of time. Predictably, he had to learn patience before he saw his first slim volume of verse in print.

The war, of course, changed everything. Rupert Brooke, confused and unhappy in love, had enrolled for the army without delay. The War Sonnets for which he is best remembered appeared in the final issue of *New Numbers* before finding more wide-spread and lasting fame on 11 March 1915 through the publication of two of them, 'The Dead' and 'The Soldier', in *The Times Literary Supplement*. Some three weeks later, 'The Soldier' was read at the Easter Sunday service at St Paul's Cathedral; and less than three weeks after that Brooke was dead, succumbing to sepsis from an infected mosquito bite on a French hospital ship moored off the island of Skyros in the Aegean. His unit was heading for the hell that would be Gallipoli; instead, he was taken ashore and buried in an olive grove, 'shielded by mountains and fragrant with sage and thyme'.

Robert Frost, revered by Thomas as a brave soul as well as a wonderful poet, wondered out loud about joining the British Army before escaping back home across the Atlantic early in 1915. His country, of course, was at that stage taking no part in the war, while expressing pro-Allies sentiments, so it would have been above and beyond the call of duty if he had taken any other course of action.

As for Edward Thomas, after Christmas, while still deep in his first infatuation with poetry, he looked back on the festive season as enjoyable 'in the modified Thomas style'. He was still busy with his literary journalism and had recently discovered the exhilaration and release of writing poems, yet even before the end of the year he was openly debating the possibility of joining up. It surprised his friends: he was 36 years old, married with children and of a studious, peaceable and melancholy nature. It had depressed him a few months previously when a gamekeeper accused Frost and him of trespassing, and the American stood up robustly to the man while he himself had simply wanted to sink into the ground. When he asked his agent what he thought of the idea of his enlisting, Charles Francis Cazenove replied: 'You startle me by saying you are not sure whether or not you should ... I should have thought your calls were elsewhere.'

Yet enlist he did, in the 28th Battalion, The London Regiment (Artists Rifles), in July 1915. With the Atlantic Ocean between him and the war zone,

Robert Frost had been making gentle fun of his friend's dithering for weeks, and it is thought that Thomas was finally pushed into action when he was sent an advance copy of 'The Road Not Taken', now one of the four-times Pulitzer prizewinning Frost's most famous poems. The American meant it as no more than an amiable chiding of what he saw as Thomas's indecision in this and other matters, but the theory is that he took it as the final push he needed. On the other hand, if Thomas had been happy in his home and personal life, it is hard to see how something like this would have been a decisive factor. After all, if he had waited for conscription, he would not have been called up until May 1916, if then.

With no thought of applying for a commission, Thomas joined as a private, was promoted to corporal, and transferred into the Royal Garrison Artillery as a second lieutenant in November 1916. He died soon after he had arrived in France; he had fought in and survived the Battle of Arras, but when it was all but over, on Easter Monday 1917, he was killed by the concussive blast of one of the last shells to be fired as he was standing lighting his pipe. He was in the wrong place at the wrong time, and there were hundreds of thousands of men in the war about whom that could be said. On the other hand, it was the lot of very few of them to leave behind a canon of creative work so memorable as the one Edward Thomas embarked upon in those inspired days of around Christmas 1914.

# REMEMBER SCARBOROUGH –
# AND HARTLEPOOL
# AND WHITBY, TOO

In the last few days before Christmas, on 16 December 1914, Britain was shaken out of what last vestiges of complacency it might have clung on to by the German naval bombardment of three communities on the north-east English coast. Hartlepool and West Hartlepool, the most northerly, could be seen as a legitimate military target. Next south came Whitby, a small fishing town that was not badly affected; and the most southerly was Scarborough, a genteel seaside resort and retirement destination for comfortably-off escapees from Leeds, Bradford and the textile towns of the West Riding.

This was the one that struck to the heart of the British people, who up until this point had taken it for granted that the war would be confined to France and Flanders, with the far-distant echoes of heavy artillery on still nights in Dover the nearest we would get to the action. But Scarborough? Why Scarborough? And if Scarborough, why not every other blameless watering-place from Filey to Bournemouth? And while we were at it, what was this wonderful British Grand Fleet of ours doing about this?

Considering what our country knew about war at first hand in 1914, the attacks had elements of the American 'shock and awe' raid on Baghdad in March 2003, designed to incapacitate and demoralise to a game-changing extent. As George W. Bush discovered then, however, there is a danger that such outrageous tactics can have the opposite effect, and serve only to strengthen the resolve of the enemy. Immediately, 'Remember Scarborough' became a rallying call; if 'Remember Belgium' had been a reminder of the danger to our homes of enemy

*War Pictures Weekly*'s artist's impression of the bombardment of Scarbrough – 'a vivid idea of the dastardly raid'. (*War Pictures Weekly*, 31 December 1914)

invasion, how much more so was the sad plight of a much-loved holiday town on our own doorsteps? Hardly surprisingly, many people in Scarborough and the other target areas were quite convinced that the attack really was the precursor of an invasion. Why should it not have been? If the Germans had wanted to land tens of thousands of troops at that moment, it was hard to see what could have stopped them.

As it was, they sailed away, and the thousands of (mainly) mothers and children who had fled – a good number of them, bizarrely, taking little more than their lovingly baked Christmas cakes with them – quickly returned to discover a viable town they still recognised, though battered and bruised in parts. Elsewhere in the country the First Lord of the Admiralty Winston Churchill, who was never short of an emotive phrase, branded the raiders 'baby-killers'. Just as significant, such is the nature of action of this kind, victims continued to die for days after the event, keeping the outrage at the top of the news agenda. 'Kaiser Scores Again' was the headline in the *Bristol Times and Mirror*, hundreds of miles from the scene, when a 6-year-old boy passed away at Christmas. The result was that young men all over the country jostled at the recruitment offices to join up. Thousands of them had already half-decided to do so after enjoying one last Christmas at home, and it was Scarborough that finally spurred them into action.

Remember Scarborough: the bombardment of a defenceless seaside resort sent shock waves throughout Britain and boosted Kitchener's recruitment drive. (LC-USZC4-11361)

To many, the episode seemed as baffling as it was disturbing. Two days before the event, British naval intelligence had picked up on a not inconsiderable task force of four battle cruisers, five light cruisers and three flotillas of destroyers heading into the North Sea from Heligoland – yet suddenly here they all were looming out of the morning mist, just a few thousand or in some cases hundreds of metres from the British shore. As we reflect in another section of this book, the full motives of the raid were unclear: was it simply to distract attention from the deadly work of a single light cruiser laying 100 mines off another Yorkshire resort, Filey, or was the aim to bring the Grand Fleet out and lure it into that ambush?

Scarborough and the two Hartlepools – today the community simply calls itself Hartlepool – were attacked almost simultaneously at around five past eight, Whitby an hour later. When the guns first started blazing, many on shore thought it was the Grand Fleet practising until they heard shells scream-ing overhead. Hartlepool's status was sensitive enough to be defended by gun batteries, but the men on watch said they had been duped by the leading battle cruiser of the three that attacked them, the *Seydiltz*, *Moltke* and *Blücher*, which was flying the British White Ensign. Such were the rudimentary communications of that time, the destroyers *Doon*, *Test*, *Waveney* and *Moy*, all based in the port, had encountered and exchanged shots with the Germans earlier, some 6 miles out, but had not somehow been able to raise the alarm. The fire from the raiders, as well as a heavy swell, also made it difficult for Hartlepool's submarine C9 or its two scout class cruisers, *Patrol* and *Forward*, to leave the harbour. As the shells rained in, the masters of *Patrol* and the sub decided to run the gauntlet and try to attack at full speed, but the cruiser was hit twice by heavy shells from *Blücher* and ran aground with four dead and seven wounded, while the sub was undamaged but unable to play a meaningful role in the battle. *Forward* was able to leave the harbour only after the Germans had sailed away.

The Hartlepool bombardment lasted some forty minutes, in which 1,150 shells were fired. The gun batteries and lighthouse, as well as a wireless station, were the principal targets, but housing nearby suffered badly, and there was little or no protection for folk going about their everyday lives. In that short time 112 men, women and children died in the town, eighty-six of them civilians, and more than 400 were injured. A shell quickly cut all lines of communication between the defending gun batteries, adding to the confusion, and others either missed their mark or were deflected into houses by the waterside. Henry Smith Terrace was very close to the firing line, and coastguards worked desperately to keep its at first inquisitive and then terrified residents out of harm's way. Even then, some of them insisted on scrambling round for shell shrapnel as souvenirs, almost before it had cooled down.

Houses in Cleveland Road, Hartlepool, devastated by
a German shell. The caption to this photograph in
*The Illustrated War News* reported, completely inaccurately:
'What should have been the chief target of the German
guns ... the battery guarding the harbour entrance, was not
struck at all.' (*The Illustrated War News*, 23 December 1914)

Seven churches, ten public buildings, five hotels
and more than 300 houses were damaged, as were
a marine engine works in the harbour and three
docked merchant ships. What struck one reporter –
and the large number of 'bombardment tourists'
who flocked around after the heat had died down –
were the beds scattered everywhere: hanging from
crumbling buildings, up on a roof, in streets and
gardens. Some had been blown through walls with
their occupants still in them.

In truth, the defences to the port were scanty, consisting of two 6-inch rapid-firing guns at the Heugh battery and a single 6-incher beside the lighthouse, each battery manned by the Durham Royal Garrison Artillery. They fired 123 rounds and inflicted damage to the *Blücher* that led to loss of life, but of course they were hopelessly outgunned: two of the German ships were armed with 11-inch guns, the cruiser *Blücher* with 8.2-inch weapons. All three of the battery guns survived the battle, but it was at the cost of nine of their crewmen dead and twelve wounded. They included Theo Jones, the first soldier to be killed on British soil in the Great War, but there were military casualties other than the battery crews. A group of Durham Territorials stationed in the town 'were standing on the sea front watching the affair as if it were a lively picnic,' according to press reports, and seven of them were killed outright by a shell.

The simultaneous raid on Scarborough had no such military objectives; a lighthouse and coastguard station took a pounding, as did the medieval castle up on its hill, and an out-of-town wireless transmitter was presumed to be another target. Other than that, it was dozens of hotels and boarding houses that bore the brunt, including the up-market Grand, as did hundreds of houses in scores of streets. The damage was more widespread than at Hartlepool but the casualty toll far lower, with seventeen dead and some eighty injured. The Grand, for instance, though a headline-grabbing target, reported no casualties among its staff or guests, who included several Yorkshire Hussars officers who did not stay off-duty for long. Not that anything could be done, other than trying to bolster the morale of a terrified town.

The battle cruisers *Derfflinger* and *Von der Tann* pounded 500 shells into the town while, as is noted elsewhere, their accomplice the light cruiser *Kolberg* was laying mines some miles south. People who had heard the commotion and gone down to the front to see what was happening watched in awe as the two ships sailed south just a few hundred metres out in the bay, their

The saloon in the Grand Hotel in Scarborough, which in its prominent position on the seafront was always a likely target. It received several hits but nobody was injured, including several army officers who were staying there. (*The Illustrated War News*, 23 December 1914)

starboard guns blazing, and then turned and repeated the exercise with their port armoury. When, an hour later, Scarborough heard their guns thundering again off Whitby, it was widely assumed that the might of the British Grand Fleet was wreaking its revenge on them.

The national press flocked to the town in the wake of this extraordinary show of force, while Scarborough's two competing weekly newspapers, the *Mercury* and the *Pictorial*, worked round the clock in a bid to out-scoop one another until well into the new year. With the *Yorkshire Post* also on the ball, local historians have been left with a rich heritage of human-interest stories.

There were the children: 'The bulk of the men in the town were out that time working, and in their absence the women and children at home were terribly frightened,' noted the *Yorkshire Post*. 'The little ones, in fact, were mostly getting up for the day, and women, some of them scantily clad, rushed into the streets, carrying troubled infants in their arms, and others crying at their skirts.' Other children, including a little girl who had run out of her house naked, were in panic because they could not find their mothers, but neighbours rallied round to take care of them. Older children were on their way to or arriving at school, and head teachers were only too pleased that the attack came just too early for them to be gathered in numbers. One school, Westlands on the exposed Filey Road, was hit, but the children had already been evacuated to its concrete-strengthened cellar. One of its pupils was a refugee from Belgium, who was quickly able to put her classmates right when they thought the clamour out in the bay was thunder. 'No, cannon!' she said, having heard it all before.

Lily Bain, aged 14 and in her last year at school, was putting her boots on and about to leave home in St John's Road when a shell burst over the house and demolished half of it, scattering shrapnel everywhere. She suffered not a scratch, though the sofa she was on was riddled with deadly shards, and her satchel and all the books in it were left in shreds. All the local press were delighted to report that her pet canary, goldfish and various puppies also lived to tell the tale.

The infant who gave Winston Churchill the chance to brand the Germans 'baby-killers' was 14-month-old John Shields Ryalls of Westbourne Park, who died a few days after a shell hit the house. The death of a 15-year-old Boy Scout, George Taylor, also struck a chord. He had gone out to buy a local newspaper as the Chief Scout, Robert Baden Powell, had visited the town the previous week, and he wanted to read the report. He died on his way to the shop.

Then there were the lucky escapes, scores of them. Police Constable Hunter was on duty at the coastguard station, which was the raiders' first target, and though he sheltered with the two coastguards, his cape was riddled with shrapnel holes and became so famous that they printed postcards of it. In fact, this being the age of the picture postcard craze, scenes of devastation in both Scarborough and Hartlepool sold in large numbers, while shells and shrapnel were also a big draw for souvenir-hunters from well beyond the locality.

A dairy horse was killed by a shell, though the milkman and his milk were left unscathed. George Scales, a merchant seaman recovering at home from a serious accident, felt a piece of shrapnel pierce his sleeve and graze his arm, but otherwise leave him undamaged, even though his peaceful recuperation was not. A young woman at communion at St Martin's church on the morning of her wedding was horrified to see shrapnel gouge a hole in the roof of the building, but still made sure that she, her groom and the vicar were back there to tie the knot three hours later. An immeasurably sadder wedding story was that of Ada Crow of Falsgrave Road and her fiancé, Sergeant Sturdy of the Indian Army. He had been away for eight-and-a-half years, and then their marriage had been postponed, first because of the outbreak of war and then after he had fallen ill. At last he got leave and arrived home on the evening of the 16th for a Christmas wedding, only to discover that his Ada had died in the Germans' fruitless attempts to demolish the wireless station near by. Her last words to her parents had been 'They're only practising'.

Four members of the Bennett family in Wykeham Street died when their home was demolished. One of the sons, Christopher, was getting dressed when his bedroom floor collapsed and tipped him into the kitchen, and it was in a dazed and injured state, dressed only in his shirt and a single sock, that he began scrambling around desperately trying to save his mother and brothers, two of them young boys. 'Would you believe it, people were laughing at him, and not one man would go up and help him,' a neighbour, Mrs Agar, told the press. 'That man is a hero. All he thought about was his mother and the others.' Christopher told the reporter: 'I had to do the best I could; if I asked one, I asked a dozen, but I couldn't see a soul to help me. There wasn't one who could come, bar two or three Territorials, who got Albert out and took him to the hospital. They were good chaps, and I shan't forget them.' In fact he did not have long to remember them: as an army driver, he was killed in action in 1917.

A local magistrate, John Hall, died when a shell struck his home in Westbourne Park. At his inquest, the coroner said of his killing and the other fatalities: 'It was a murderous attack which caused these deaths, a murderous attack on an unfortified town, and all the world should know.' Another desperate story was that of Mrs Duffield of Esplanade Road. Her husband thought the danger was over when the guns fell silent as the ships turned halfway through their mission, and set off to a local boarding house to telephone the fire station. As soon as the bombardment started up again, his wife ran out to make sure he was all right, only to be cut down by a shell. The saddest irony of all, of course, was that by this time the fire brigade was all too aware of what was going on. Then there was Mrs Merryweather, whose shop at the corner of Prospect Road had a stout cellar; she and her husband were making for it when at the last minute she decided to go out and invite some friends to share it with them, only to die of shrapnel wounds.

Later statistics showed that it had been far safer to stay at home rather than out on the street. The *Derfflinger* and *Von der Tann* had 12-inch guns and 11-inch guns respectively as their main weapons, each despatching shells that weighed a ton. At Scarborough, however, they saw the need to use only 5.9-inch and 6.9-inch weapons, the speculation being that they were saving the big guns for an expected encounter with the British Grand Fleet.

The following summer of 1915 brought an influx of curious visitors, and when they complained that there did not seem to be much to see any more, a photographic exhibition was set up at a big house on Filey Road, Dunollie, where two servants had died in the raid. Then there were the rumours: Mr Bell of Burniston was suddenly convinced the distinguished elderly gent he had met on the road near his home the day before the raid was a German spy, even though, at the time, he had taken him to be a Scotsman. 'You'll be safe here behind that rising ground when the Germans come,' the man had said. 'The Germans'll never come here,' Mr Bell replied.

'But they will, and quickly, too, you'll see.' An odd encounter, it must be admitted, but in other ways the speculation all got quickly out of hand.

A respected local shopkeeper, James Gagen, was charged under the Defence of the Realm Consolidation Act, 1914, for spreading a false report after he had said that 'German ships were sighted off Hull and Newcastle, and our ships dare not go out to fight them.' Tittle-tattle, no more or less, but the authorities wanted to nip it in the bud, and poor old Mr G. was the scape-goat. 'The military was determined that any person who was caught spreading such reports would be dealt with, otherwise chaos would ensue,' the *Scarborough Mercury* reported on Christmas Eve. 'This was "idle gossip, and foolishness". In the event he was discharged, but the court reminded everyone that the military could have ordered a court martial, in which case he was liable to be sentenced to penal servitude for life.'

Then there had been the visit to Scarborough in August 1913 of the German passenger steamship *Kronprinzessin Cecilie*, apparently full of delegates who had been to an international medical confer-ence. They were welcomed warmly, with the women presented with flowers and chocolates – but then the doubts began to creep in. Had they not been a bit too keen to learn about the coastguards, the castle, the lighthouse and the harbour? Some of these so-called doctors had not seemed to be able to answer some fairly simple medical questions, had they? A local lad who spoke German reckoned he overheard one of them say the castle 'could easily be taken'. Then there was the lofty Red House in Falsgrave, with its open aspect to the sea. Had there been signals going out from there? After all, a German family had lived there as recently as a mere twenty years ago!

Leaving Scarborough to ponder its undeserved fate, the *Derfflinger* and *Von der Tann* then steamed full-speed for Whitby, when the shelling began at five past nine and lasted no more than seven minutes. More than 100 missiles hit the town in that time, however, wrecking about thirty houses and killing two men. The *Scarborough Mercury* reported unflinchingly that Frederick Randall, a coastguard, 'died as he was putting up the White Ensign – a shell burst near by, blowing his head clean off'. The other victim was an elderly railwayman who was driving a horse and cart near the station when a small shell struck him. This time, reversing the Scarborough milk float story, it was the horse that was unhurt.

'Other persons came off comparatively lightly with cuts and bruises,' the *Mercury* continued. 'In some cases nearly the whole front of the house was torn away, and in others the shell fell on the roof and bored a gaping passage down to the kitchen floor. Furniture of all kinds was smashed, and crockery became non-existent. In one case a projectile fell upon a bed which a young woman had occupied only a short time before.' This time, in contrast to Scarborough, it seems

The coastguard station at Whitby, where one of the coastguards died. (*The Illustrated War News*, 23 December 1914)

that at least some 11-inch shells were used, making holes in fields 'large enough to bury horses in'.

And then came the great escape. Six hours after the raid a trawler skipper said he had been passed by six German battleships hightailing it back to Heligoland: 'I never saw warships travelling so fast before.' Earl Jellicoe was ordered by the Admiralty to send vessels from Scapa and Cromarty to try to intercept, but the Scapa contingent in particular was handicapped by stormy weather, to the extent that two light cruisers returned heavily damaged by the sea and with several men washed overboard and lost. This brief glimpse of a tiny footnote of the war is a reminder of just how expendable manpower had become, of the new-found cheapness of human life.

Farther east in the North Sea, British squadrons did draw close to the fleeing Germans, but by this time poor visibility was adding to their problems. In truth, neither side was spoiling for a fight in such an ad hoc manner. Sea battles were a risky business, and no commander

The picture the press had been waiting for: the sinking of the *Blücher*, one of the Hartlepools' assailants, at Dogger Bank in January 2015. (*War Pictures Weekly*, 4 February 1915)

wished to be thrown into a situation without meticulous forward-planning. What the British did not know was that far more of the German fleet was out on the high seas that day than intelligence reports had picked up on. If the fleeing warships had been engaged, the Grand Fleet might have met stiffer resistance than it had bargained for. Better to win the overall war at sea than risk all to satisfy the outcry for immediate revenge.

As events turned out, the jingoistic headline-writers did not have to wait long for their moment. In January 1915, a German raiding party, including several of the 16 December vessels, was intercepted at Dogger Bank, apparently heading for Tyneside. It immediately turned for home, but to great press acclaim the comparatively slow *Blücher*, one of the scourges of Hartlepool, was sunk as it tried to escape a British battle squadron led by Rear Admiral David Beatty's flagship the *Lion*. Also badly damaged were the *Moltke* from the Hartlepool encounter and the *Derfflinger*, one of the two battle cruisers that had terrorised Scarborough. Both were ablaze, entirely incapacitated as a fighting force and suffering from serious loss of manpower, but somehow they continued to limp towards home. Beatty kept up the chase until an ominous-looking Zeppelin and several aircraft hove into view, and he backed off. Zeppelins had still not played a significant part in this conflict, but their pre-war reputation had gone before them; tactically aggressive as he famously was, the old sea dog was taking no chances.

# Business as Usual in Country Courtrooms

Britain was facing undreamed-of perils by land, sea and air, her young men were going through hell and fighting and dying like heroes in 'the war to end all wars'. Yet for grassroots police officers and magistrates up and down the land there was an irksomely familiar pattern to life, as these court reports from rural Gloucestershire in December 1914 make plain:

Edward Basil, leather-cutter from Nailsworth, was summoned for refusing to quit the Shears Inn, Nailsworth on 5 December. Frank Holborrow, the licensee, said that the defendant, after being in the house twenty minutes, and having been served with a pint of beer, accused him of having half-a-crown belonging to him. This he asked for and refused to leave without it. Witness sent for the police. Police Constable Spragg spoke of being called to the house, where he found the landlord and defendant having a scuffle together. Defendant was fined 5s.

Anthony Thomas Grice, of Nailsworth, was summoned for keeping a dangerous dog on 11 December. Superintendent Briggs observed that all that was required was either that the dog be destroyed or be kept under proper control. Edward Fryer Smith of Overdean, Nailsworth, said that on the day in question he and his wife entered a shop in Nailsworth when the dog 'flew' at his wife and tore her dress. It afterwards got hold of the witness and drew blood. Inspector Brotheridge spoke of having received several complaints about the dog and the defendant was ordered to keep the dog under control and pay the costs of the court, viz. 6s.

Peter Day, labourer of Horsley, was fined 6d and 4s 6d costs for damaging windows, the property of Charles Hurn, on 6 December. Defendant admitted breaking one pane accidentally. Prosecutor said that defendant, who used disgraceful language and wanted to fight, first of all broke an upstairs window with an iron bar, and then threw the bar through a downstairs window.

Edward Hanks, labourer of Horsley, was summoned by his wife Alice for assault on 12 December. Complainant said that her husband, who staggered indoors at dinnertime, struck her on the shoulder with his hand. She had previously had a separation order against him. Defendant, who did not appear, was fined 10s and 1s 6d costs.

Mary Lamb of Walls Quarry, Brimscombe, applied for a separation order against her husband, John William Lamb, on account of alleged physical cruelty. Applicant said her husband was always causing upset at home, and about a week ago he told her to clear out. Taking him at his word, she left him. Defendant said he was willing to take his wife back again, and the bench therefore dismissed the case, advising the parties to make it up again.

Felix David Willett, a shop assistant of Cecil Road, Gloucester, was charged with obtaining by false pretences £6 1s, the monies of Elizabeth Ball, of Tower Hill, Stroud, on 22 November, with intent to defraud her of the same. Prosecutrix, a widow, said the prisoner, who was a stranger to her, had been lodging at her house since the middle of September. On 12 November he told her that his mother was very ill and had been sent to the Gloucestershire Workhouse Infirmary. He said she was suffering from cancer and dropsy, but did not then ask for any money.

Later, her told her his mother had passed away during the night of the 14th. He said 'I don't know what I shall do for expenses', and after going to work returned a short time later and asked the witness to let him have what money she could, her daughter having told him her mother would lend him a shilling or two. Witness lent him £5, prisoner stating that he had £21 to come from his mother, the amount of her insurance. He also said he had £50 to come from his own insurance, but had to pay all his mother's debts. He said his aunt had given him £8, and his two sisters had had £12. On the following Tuesday he paid her back the £5, and on 22 November he asked her for £6, which he let him have.

Police Constable Pointon said he saw prisoner's mother on Friday, 18 December, when she was alive and well. When he arrested prisoner he made the following statement, which he signed: 'She said to me "David, if ever you want any money you can have some", and said it would do till a month or two after Christmas.' Police Sergeant Spicer asked for a remand until Thursday and this was granted, bail being refused.

John Rawlings, a tailor of Bowbridge, Stroud, was charged with using threats towards his wife, Maude Rawlings, on 25 December. Complainant said between eleven and twelve o'clock of the morning in question prisoner was sitting by the fire and asked the eldest daughter to cut him some food, but she did not hear him, and he took up the fire tongs and threatened to kill her. The prisoner told the witness that if she interfered he would hit her brains out also. She was then so afraid that she went out and fetched the police.

She was afraid he would do her some injury, and told the court that for several years her life had been a misery. He had been ill for some time, and neither she nor the children dared to speak above a whisper. Gwennie Rawlings, daughter of the prisoner, corroborated. Police Constable Aston spoke of going to the house, having been called by the complainant, and he endeavoured to persuade them to 'make it up'. In the witness box, prisoner said the whole cause of the trouble was because he asked the daughter to cut him some food, and that she became cheeky to him. He denied having used the threats. Prisoner was bound over in the sum of £5 to keep the peace for six months towards both his wife and children.

# MARK SHERIDAN, THE TRAGIC TROUPER

There would never be a time like Christmas 1914 and the weeks leading up to it for the music-hall star Mark Sheridan, who cashed in on the country's mood of wild optimism with two flag-waving songs with choruses so catchy that one of them – 'Here We Are Again' – is still known to many of us today. Maybe we can be excused for being a little vague on the other one, though its splendid title, 'Belgium Put The Kibosh On The Kaiser', surely deserves to be remembered a little more fondly than it is. When it was featured in the musical *Oh! What a Lovely War* in 1963, and its film version six years later, most of the audience simply took it to be a modern ironic parody.

Sheridan had struck gold before, with 'I Do Like To Be Beside The Seaside' in 1909, which again caught the spirit of the times by celebrating the myth or reality of those golden Edwardian summers. As 1914 drew to an end, however, the mood was on the turn, and audiences who had raised the roof with 'Are we downhearted? No!!' in 'Here We Are Again' in September were distinctly more sotto voce after the excitement of Christmas had faded away. Suddenly Mark Sheridan's up-beat jingoism was not what was wanted, and before the end of the war he had taken his own life, feeling isolated and rejected by his public.

How different it was back in September 1914, when the showbiz paper *The Era* reported:

> At the Oxford [Theatre, London] on Monday night Mr Mark Sheridan introduced a new song, 'Here We Are Again', the music by Kenneth Lyle, with words by Charles Knight, which proved to be an instantaneous success. The melody was so catchy that the crowded audience took it up at once, and sang it lustily ... The song bids fair to rival the far more famous 'It's A Long, Long Way To Tipperary', as it has just the kind of lilt likely to appeal to soldiers on the march ...

In November, Sheridan was at the heart of a patriotic week at the Empire in his (almost) home town of Sunderland, when the management handed the profits of nearly £600 to the mayor's local war relief fund, he passed on his week's salary of £175, his wife donated ten guineas and his sale of signed photographs brought in another £26. On the Wednesday he headed a remarkable patriotic matinee in which a bill that included such substantial names of the day as Wee Georgie Wood, Zona Vevey and Max Erard, Walter Passmore and Agnes Fraser, Nora Delany, Gus Garrick, Madge Allan and the juggler Frank Hartley performed for free. A few days before Christmas Sheridan had come south to one of his favourite stamping grounds, the Victoria Palace in London, where *The Era* foresaw a tumultuous welcome for 'Here We Are Again' and 'Kibosh'. And so it proved.

Mark Sheridan, known on his bill matter as 'The Wise Jester' or 'One Of The B'hoys', was born Fred Shaw in Hendon, County Durham in 1864 of Scottish-Irish parents. His first work was on Sunderland Docks, and he was delighted to get an office job at the Newcastle-upon-Tyne Theatre before realising that his place was on stage. In many ways he was an identikit music-hall performer – odd looks, daft patter, adept dancing and singing – but he was different and slick enough to break into the London and national circuit in 1895, after extensive tours of South Africa and Australia, and very few people on the halls had a defter ear for a catchy song. Pantomime was another of his great strengths – but his health was a problem, with several writers after his death speculating on various nervous disorders.

Yes, Christmas 1914 was the zenith of Sheridan's career, and with enthusiasm for not only patriotic songs but music hall itself on the wane by 1915, his thoughts began to turn to revue, combining music, dance and sketches with a topical and satirical twist.

His first taste of it saw him starring in a lengthy tour of a show called *Winkles*, and by 1917 he felt confident enough with the concept to write, compose and direct a production of his own. *Gay Paree*, based on W.G. Wills's West End hit *A Royal Divorce*, cost £2,000 to produce with its company of forty, elaborate sets and costumes. He had staked a lot on it, and to him it was imperative that it should succeed.

It had been touring for less than a month when it opened at Glasgow Coliseum on 14 January 1918. He chose the venue especially because they had always loved him there, pouring their adoration out to him. It was not quite like that at the two performances that night; he seemed in good form and got his laughs, but he knew it was not like the glory days. It was the same when the Glasgow papers came out the following day. They were not anything like hostile, but they were not ecstatic, either. Unrestrained laughter can be like a drug to comedians, and when it dries up, the whole world takes on a darker hue.

Later that day two men walking in Kelvingrove Park found the body of a man – a grotesque sight, with a bullet wound in his forehead and a Browning revolver lying beside him. When police came along they knew instantly who it was. Mark Sheridan was 53.

But begone, dull care. The B'hoy always prided himself on sending 'em out laughing, and to sample what they were laughing at 100 years ago, here is a reminder

of the first two verses and chorus of 'Belgium Put
The Kibosh On The Kaiser'. Be warned: there are many,
many more of them if you want to seek them out ...

A silly German sausage
Dreamt Napoleon he'd be,
Then he went and broke his promise,
It was made in Germany.
He shook hands with Britannia
And eternal peace he swore,
Naughty boy, he talked of peace
While he prepared for war.

He stirred up little Serbia
To serve his dirty tricks
But naughty nights at Liege
Quite upset this Dirty Dick.
His luggage labelled 'England'
And his programme nicely set,
He shouted 'First stop Paris',
But he hasn't got there yet.

**Chorus:** For Belgium put the kibosh on the Kaiser;
Europe took the stick and made him sore;
On his throne it hurts to sit,
And when John Bull starts to hit,
He will never sit upon it any more.

# 'A MAN WHOSE STRONG HEART STILL BEATS LOUDLY'

On 21 December 1914, Walter Daniel John Tull exchanged one extraordinary pioneering career for another. Quite where his multiple talents might have led him had he survived the war is anybody's guess. Britain's first black MP? Probably not, since it was 1987 before that rubicon was crossed, but he would certainly have made his mark in some significant way.

The son of a Barbadian carpenter and his Kentish wife, Walter Tull was born in Folkestone in 1888, at first had a happy childhood but had lost both parents by the time he was 9. He and his brother Edward were brought up in a Methodist orphanage in Bethnal Green, London, and it was there that his sporting prowess came to the fore. When he was 20 he was catching the football press's eye as an inside forward for Clapton in the Isthmian League, and in his first season he helped them to the treble of the FA Amateur Cup and the London County Amateur and Senior Cups.

It was the kind of feat that had everyone sitting up and taking notice, and when Clapton's upwardly mobile neighbours Tottenham Hotspur were promoted to the First Division for the first time at the end of that 1908–09 season they offered Tull a contract that turned him into England's second mixed-race professional footballer after Arthur Wharton, a goalkeeper at Darlington and Rotherham.

His time at the top was brief. He played in Spurs' opening match of 1909–10, at Sunderland, but made only another nine first-team appearances. He was certainly good enough for the elite league, and it is now widely accepted that, shockingly, racial abuse was his downfall. There was a particularly unhappy afternoon at Bristol City, when it was reported that 'a section of the spectators made a cowardly attack on him in language lower than Billingsgate'. The correspondent continued: 'Let me tell those Bristol hooligans that Tull is so clean in mind and method as to be a model for all white men who play football, whether they be amateur or professional. In point of ability, if not actual achievement, Tull was the best forward on the field.'

In October 1911 he moved on to the calmer waters of the Southern League, where Herbert Chapman, before his legendary success as manager of Huddersfield Town and Arsenal, brought him in in exchange for a 'substantial fee' and the accomplished full-back Charlie Brittain. Tull quickly

Walter Tull, pioneer in the fields of sport and war.
(Phil Vasili)

became a mainstay of the Northampton Town team, switching to half-back and playing in more than 100 games before the First World War. He set an example to all his teammates by being the first to join up that December, enlisting in the Middlesex Regiment's famous Footballers' Battalion, the 17th, as its fifty-fifth member. He went on to fight in the regiment's 23rd Battalion before his war came to its unhappy end.

It was in the army that he made history for the second time in his short life, commissioned in the Special Reserve of Officers in May 1917, in defiance of the 1914 Manual of Military Law's decree that 'aliens [including "persons of colour"] must not exercise any actual command or power'. It was as the service's first black commissioned infantry officer that Second Lieutenant Tull died at the second Battle of the Somme on 25 March 1918, a month before his thirtieth birthday. He was shot while leading an attack on the German trenches at Favreuil, and his men thought so highly of him that several made valiant efforts to bring him back to their trenches under heavy fire. In the event, his body was never recovered.

Earlier he had fought five major battles in France and Flanders, including both Somme offensives, while in Italy he was cited by his commander for his for 'gallantry and coolness' after leading his company of twenty-six men on a night raid across the swift-flowing River Piave and returning them all unharmed. That, in January 1918, led to his being recommended for the Military Cross, but two months later he was dead. Years on, a Glasgow newspaper reported that had he lived, he would have resumed his football career with Rangers. Some kind of bond might have been forged in 1916, when Tull was briefly sent home from the front line through illness but had then been recommended for officer training at Gailes, Ayrshire, where the links were and still are owned and managed by Glasgow Golf Club.

Walter Tull's name is numbered among those with no known grave on the Arras Memorial, while Northampton Town honoured him in 1999 with a memorial at their Sixsmiths Stadium, as well as naming an approach road after him. The epitaph on the memorial was written by Phil Vasili, the author of *Walter Tull, 1888–1918, Officer, Footballer: 'All the guns in France couldn't wake me'* (Raw Press, 2009). It reads:

> Through his actions, Tull ridiculed the barriers of ignorance that tried to deny people of colour equality with their contemporaries. His life stands testament to a determination to confront those people and those obstacles that sought to diminish him and the world in which he lived. It reveals a man, though rendered breathless in his prime, whose strong heart still beats loudly.

The large number of footballers of all races in modern British football has stimulated interest in the pioneers of diversity in the sport, and Tull's name is now more widely known than it has been for generations. There are plans to put up a statue in his memory at Tottenham Hotspur's eventual new ground, his life was the subject of a BBC Four docu-drama in 2008 and there is the possibility of a full-length feature film scripted by Mr Vasili. Two books for children have been written, as well as teachers' guides.

Phil Vasili is also at the heart of 'Crossing the White Line: The Walter Tull Story', an award-winning website he has put together with the City of Westminster Archives, with funding from the Kick it Out campaign, the Heritage Lottery and other smaller donors. It tells a story that would have been remarkable even if it had ended at the outbreak of the First World War – but became truly extraordinary after Walter Tull had stepped into the unknown and taken the decision to answer his country's call four days before Christmas 1914.

# THE CHRISTMAS
# NUMBER ONE

The title is misleading. It would be the best part of forty years before Britain had a meaningful pop chart, and a couple of decades after that before the question of who happened to be top of the heap on 25 December came to be seen as of any significance. Nevertheless, popular songs there were aplenty for troops in and around the trenches to have buzzing through their heads in idle hours and maybe even in the heat of battle.

'It's A Long, Long Way To Tipperary' and its like were high on the agenda, of course, but in there was also a lot of music that might surprise us today. Some of it was pure music hall – Harry Lauder, Vesta Tilley, Marie Lloyd, George Robey, imported hits from vaudeville across the Atlantic; but also from America in the first years of the new century had come ragtime, with its ragged, syncopated beat sending shock waves through a public brought up on singalongs and parlour songs, while the West End and Broadway's burgeoning musical comedy scene was also rich in melody. It was all change on the musical scene, and some of that would have filtered through to the industrial towns, if not so much to the country villages.

> We are Fred Karno's army, the ragtime infantry.
> We cannot fight, we cannot shoot, what bleedin' use are we?

The lads roared, rather undermining their ragtime credentials by singing it to the tune of one of the classic hymns, 'The Church's One Foundation Is Jesus Christ Her Lord.'

Songs the boys at the front in 1914 grew up with which are still known to many today included 'Daisy Bell', the one about looking sweet upon the seat of a bicycle made for two, 'Cuddle Up A Little Closer, Lovey Mine', 'Give My Regards To Broadway', 'In The Good Old Summer Time', 'In The Shade Of The Old Apple Tree', 'Oh You Beautiful Doll', 'Shine On Harvest Moon' and the knockabout 'He'd Have To Get Under', chronicling the woes of Johnny O'Connor in his thwarted attempts to do a spot of spooning in his new-fangled motorcar:

> He'd have to get under, get out and get under
> To fix his little machine,
> He was just dying to cuddle his queen,
> But ev'ry minute,
> When he'd begin it,
> He'd have to get under, get out and get under,
> Then he'd get back at the wheel

A dozen times they'd start to hug and kiss
And then the darned old engine, it would miss
And then he'd have to get under, get out and get under
And fix up his automobile.

It all ended up with his sweetie sitting on his knee and him driving into a tree, and it is not surprising that young men who could no more afford a car than fly to the moon took the song to their hearts: for the have-nots, the fact that early motor transport was notoriously unreliable was a comforting source of schadenfreude, while the constant woes of transports stuck in the mud behind the trenches gave the words added irony as the war dragged on. Among artists who recorded the song in 1913 and 1914 were Al Jolson and Billy Murray, 'The Denver Nightingale', who could be said to be the first great pop star of the twentieth century.

Another, very different Billy Murray song was 'I Wonder Who's Kissing Her Now', from the 1909 Broadway musical *The Prince of Tonight*:

I wonder who's kissing her now,
I wonder who's teaching her how,
Wonder who's looking into her eyes,
Breathing sighs, telling lies;
I wonder who's buying the wine,
For lips that I used to call mine.
I wonder if she ever tells him of me,
I wonder who's kissing her now.

This, of course, strikes chords far more profound and unsettling than the urge to make fun of toffs having trouble with their cars, and it is surely no surprise that it was equally in the minds of that next generation of fighting men two decades down the line; not a morale-booster, anything but, but a potent reminder that there was another life out there, however much the shells and bombs and machine guns were trying to prove otherwise. Besides, in the First World War rather more than the Second, most married men at the front had just cause to believe that nobody much other than their babies and children were kissing her now.

Several songs that stood the test of time, not quite until today in some cases, but for decades, were among the hits of the last couple of years before the war: 'Moonlight Bay', 'I'm Twenty-One Today', 'Waiting For The Robert E Lee', 'When You Were Sweet Sixteen', 'Ragtime Cowboy Joe', 'Who Were You With Last Night?' and 'Everybody's Doing It Now', all in 1912; and in 1913, 'When Irish Eyes Are Smiling', 'Peg O' My Heart', 'The Spaniard Who Blighted My Life', 'Row! Row! Row!', 'The Trail Of The Lonesome Pine', 'When The Midnight Choo-Choo Leaves For Alabam', 'You Made Me Love You', 'Ballin' The Jack' and Harry Lauder's 'It's Nicer To Be In Bed'. Then, in 1914, in the last months of peace, emerged such contrasting evergreens as 'They Didn't Believe Me', 'Keep The Home Fires Burning', 'Hello, Who's Your Lady Friend?', 'Aba Daba Honeymoon', 'Colonel Bogey', 'Play A Simple Melody' and 'I Hear Music'.

'They Didn't Believe Me', a classic from the Great American Songbook that again did sterling service in the Second World War, was Jerome Kern's first major success, with lyrics by Herbert Reynolds. The pair had been asked to write five new songs when the musical *The Girl From Utah* transferred from the West End to Broadway, and the theatre historian John Kenrick sees this one as the first great modern show tune, abandoning waltz-time for the four beats to a bar of the foxtrot, and putting everyday language ahead of the poetic, especially in its verses. The song grew even less poetic by the time the Tommies had finished with it:

> And when they ask us,
> How dangerous it was,
> Oh, we'll never tell them,
> No, we'll never tell them.
> We spent our pay in some café
> And fought wild women every day,
> 'Twas the cushiest job we ever had ...

The author of this book knows from first-hand experience how this version of the song survived into the 1960s, along with cod French phrases such as 'toot-sweet', 'san fairy ann' and 'parley-voo'. The original was one of his mother's favourite romantic love songs, which she would always sing with feeling when she was busy around the house. A school friend, on the other hand, would sometimes sing snatches of this more ribald take on the song, presumably passed down to him by some uncle or grandfather. There seems something dark about this version, going beyond the men's laudable wish to shield their loved ones from the horrors of what they had seen; it is symbolic of the way the war drove a wedge between relationships, and of how women's attempts to sympathise with and ease the pain of their returning menfolk were all too often met with scorn and irritation. Married couples tended to stay married, because that was what married couples did in those days; but large numbers of sweet and loving young girlfriends of the pre-war years, whom the men would have been happy to have made their wives in normal circumstances, were cruelly cast aside: 'You understand? How the hell could you possibly understand?'

Of course, there were other song parodies aplenty in the trenches, often concerning women, not surprisingly. 'Tipperary' gave the lads:

> There's only one way to tickle Mary,
> And we learned it over here.

And then there was the newly written 'Sous Les Ponts De Paris', a tune that suddenly seemed to be played everywhere behind the lines in that bal-musette accordion style which we still hear today in films and instantly think 'This is supposed to be France'.

The Tommies had a version of it that tells of the sense of loss the French girls will feel when the boys go home, and how they will cry:

> Apres la guerre fini,
> Soldat Anglais parti,
> Mamselle Fransay boko pleuray,
> Apres la guerre fini.

The third line of the second verse tells how she will be in the family way, while in the third verse:

> Mademoiselle can go to hell,
> Apres la guerre fini.

Again, it is a callous, unfeeling song born of a callous, unfeeling world, and forty years later, in the mid-1950s, it must have come as a great surprise for a good many men approaching retirement age when that haunting melody last heard in some seedy little bar best forgotten re-emerged from the shadows as a mainstream pop song, 'Under The Bridges Of Paris'.

In fact it is surprising how many of those songs of 1914 enjoyed a resurgence in the middle years of the century – even the daft 'Aba Daba Honeymoon', which reported faithfully the gibberish conversation between a love-struck monkey and a chimpanzee. 'The nadir of all American expression', the novelist Thomas Pynchon called it, but after it had been showcased in the 1950 film *Two Weeks With Love*, three versions of it reached the US charts, including a No. 3 for Debbie Reynolds and Carleton Carpenter.

The 'Colonel Bogey March', finished in the last few weeks of peacetime, was the work of the army bandmaster Lieutenant Frederick J. Ricketts, who wrote as Kenneth J. Alford to keep separate his official work and his composing (and presumably royalty cheques). He always said the tune was inspired by an old golfer he knew who whistled a characteristic two-note musical phrase instead of shouting 'Fore!', and it was also golf that gave the song its name.

In 1890 the secretary of Coventry Golf Club came up with the idea of standardising the number of shots a good golfer should take at each hole, which he called the ground score. The idea spread, and in a match play competition at Great Yarmouth one day one of the players, frustrated by his opponent's consistency at every hole, called him 'a regular Bogeyman' after a menacing character in a music-hall song of the time:

Hush-hush-hush,
Here comes the Bogeyman!
Don't let him come too close to you,
He'll catch you if he can ...

The upshot was that at Yarmouth and elsewhere the ground score became known as the Bogey score, with Mister Bogey the imaginary opponent who never faltered. This was all very well at most clubs, but when Colonel Seely-Vidal, the honorary secretary of the United Services Club at Gosport, worked out the ground score for his course, he was faced with a dilemma. Mere 'Misters' had no place at the USC; everybody had a military rank – and so, suddenly, did Colonel Bogey. The reason par became the ground score and bogey took on the meaning of one over par was not a nicety that much concerned the lads in the trenches at Christmas 1914, and it is not one that should trouble us here.

As for Lieutenant Ricketts, his last posting was as director of music for the Royal Marines at Plymouth, where he wrote a further twenty or so marches. They were good, some say as good as Sousa's; but apart from 'Colonel Bogey', none became a sheet music million-seller – or lived on into the next world war to serve as a major morale-booster for servicemen and more ribald civilians alike, with dubious added words speculating on the physical attributes, or rather non-attributes, of Germany's Führer.

Irving Berlin's 'Play A Simple Melody' came from his first stage musical, *Watch Your Step*, in 1914. Of course it has been revived many times since, and its two distinct melodies intertwined in counterpoint, sweet and sour, pioneered a musical device that was still working well far into the century. In fact Berlin himself repeated the exercise twice in his long career, first in *Call Me Madam* with 'You're

Just In Love' in 1950 and then, more than fifty years after 1914, with 'An Old-Fashioned Wedding' for the 1966 revival of his *Annie Get Your Gun*. What does change over the decades is the dynamic: in 1914 it was the female lead who was the dreamy one, while she is the feisty realist in the two later songs.

Another aspect of 'Play A Simple Melody' was its hot topicality:

> Musical demon, set your honey a-dreamin'
> Won't you play me some rag?

Runs the syncopated counterpoint, and in 1914 you did not get much more on-the-ball than that. It was as if Berlin was saying 'All right, ragtime might be all the rage and from a world very different from mine, but don't worry. If that's what you want I can dish that up too, no problem.'

Traditionally the popularity of songs had been gauged by sheet-music sales, and at the beginning of the First World War that was still the case; but now all the best-sellers were finding their way on to records, 78rpm shellac discs, and in the post-war years, with mass-produced gramophones revolutionising home entertainment, they would become the touchstone by which success was measured. Apart from anything else, with jazz following ragtime as the big musical craze of the 1920s, who wanted sheet music, with all that bewildering tangle of notes?

From late Victorian times advances had been made in recording on both cylinder and disc, and in terms of quality there was not a lot to choose between the two. As in the VHS-Betamax video format war of the late 1970s and early '80s, however, critical commercial factors came into play, and increasingly apparent economies in disc production prompted an at first reluctant Edison company to put its weight behind that medium in 1912. That having been said, the company continued to produce cylinders in tandem with some 10-inch records until 1929.

Oddly, for the lads at the front on both sides, a gramophone was not the impossible dream it might be imagined to be. There are many accounts of wind-up models finding their way out there, along with musical instruments, and the strains of favourite songs wafting over no-man's-land to the enemy's trenches at night. Nevertheless, as in the music halls back home, it was word of mouth that taught the troops many of the songs that were closest to their hearts. Part of the music-hall tradition, naturally, was for the audience to join in with the chorus long and loud, and that was the way the soldiers knew and understood their music. Community singing was a fact of life, as it remained into the 1950s and '60s, when social evenings and coach trips would still frequently end in a sing-song. At the beginning of the war the boys really were singing 'It's A Long, Long Way To Tipperary', as the song was first named in 1912, with that extra 'Long', while by the end of 1914 Ivor Novello's 'Keep The Home Fires Burning' had been added to the repertoire. 'Pack Up Your Troubles In Your Old Kit Bag' followed in 1915.

Another song rarely recalled these days but often mentioned by troops in their letters home was 'Billy Muggins'. 'The Bosch were singing "Tipperary", but we sang "Billy Muggins" back to them,' one of them noted after a far-from-isolated friendly exchange in the first few months of the war. This music-hall song performed by Charles R. Whittle, the 'Let's All Go Down The Strand' man, tells the story of one of those singular, quiet types who are not nearly as daft as they are taken to be. In four verses and choruses he tells how his workmates waste their money in the pub while he goes home and has some grub; how friends asked him round to play cards, thinking they would fleece him, but he ended up going home with ten sovereigns; and how his brother is sued for breach of promise, but while Billy had courted the same young woman, he had had his way with her but got away with it because:

> When she said love letters gave her delight
> Why did I tell her I could not write?

We shall let the last verse and chorus, always a great favourite with the lads in the trenches, speak for themselves:

I never stay out late at night, I never want to roam
My landlady is good to me, so Muggins stops at home
My landlord thinks it only right for him to stop out late
    at night
Why does he leave a chap like me to keep his
    missus company?

I'm Billy Muggins, commonly known as a Juggins
Silly Billy, that's what my friends call me
Why does my landlady call me a dear
Treat me to smokes and to bottles of beer?
I'm Muggins the Juggins, and Muggins I'll always be.

Another soldier, writing home after the Christmas truce of 1914, reported that while the Germans sang 'O Tannenbaum', he and his mates replied with 'We Are Fred Karno's Army'. Like 'Billy Muggins', this is a self-deprecating song with a twist, because in real life Billy has very much got his head screwed on the right way, while when 'Fred Karno's Army' gets to Berlin it will give the Kaiser a fright. Both are jokey, streetwise songs, compared with the Germans' straight renditions of 'Tipperary' and 'O Tannenbaum'. On the other hand, when the troops told of such exchanges of songs, it was rarely with any malice towards Fritz.

It is unlikely that the troops and sailors at the sharp end were sitting around warbling the jingoistic, tub-thumping choruses that came out in a plethora at the beginning of the war, but there is no doubt that many of them had been influenced by those urgent tunes in being pushed over the edge to join up, either directly or as a result of the febrile atmosphere the songs had partly helped to engender up and down the country.

Within almost days of the outbreak of hostilities two songs with the title 'Your King and Country Need You' and another substituting 'Want' for 'Need' were doing the rounds of the halls – all catchy, all capturing the spirit of get-up-and-at-'em patriotism of the time, and all expressing sentiments it was very easy to sing about if you were not going to be the one trudging up the troop ship's gangway with your kit bag on your shoulder.

> Come on Tommy, come on Jack,
> We'll guard the home till you come back,
> Come on Sandy, come on Pat,
> For you're true blue!
> Down your tools and leave your benches,
> Say goodbye to all the wenches,
> Take your gun, and may God speed you!
> For your King and Country need you!

This was the chorus of the 'Need You' song written by Paul Pelham, the publishers of which donated half the profits on the first 100,000 copies of sheet music to the Prince of Wales's National Relief Fund.

It is the chorus of the 'Want You' number that is best remembered today, however, with words and music written by Paul Rubens as a 'woman's recruiting song' to be sung with the aim of persuading or shaming men to volunteer. The profits from this one were given to Queen Mary's Work for Women Fund, but its wording was very soon modified to be sung equally by men of the kind who, for whatever reason, felt safe in their belief that it was not directed towards them. The chorus, of course, was:

Oh! We don't want to lose you,
But we think you ought to go,
For your King and Country,
Both need you so.
We shall want you and miss you,
But with all our might and main.
We shall cheer you, thank you, kiss (bless) you,
When you come back again.

The composer Rubens had a string of London shows to his credit and had written additional material – including 'A Maid's Career Is Skittles And Beer' – for *Floradora*, the first big West End hit to take Broadway by storm. Rubens did not heed his own call to take up arms, but on the other hand, he was 39 and chronically ill when the war began and died of TB early in 1917. For some years he was engaged to the stunning actress Phyllis Dare and worked with her on some of the most glittering West End shows of the time, but it all fell apart when his condition forced him to retreat to Cornwall. We must accept that, far away from the front, he did not enjoy an easy war.

'All The Boys In Khaki Get The Nice Girls' was another early favourite, but the tone of music-hall war numbers changed as the fighting wore on. 'Roses Of Picardy', published in 1916, was a pretty, sentimental love song written by the Bath-based King's Counsel Fred Weatherly, with music by Haydn Wood. Weatherly could be as tough as old boots in the courtroom, but even in these changing musical times he proved that there was still a place for parlour songs, as he had shown six years earlier when he transformed the traditional 'Londonderry Air' into 'Danny Boy'.

A more rousing song, though by now acknowledging the sheer, grinding monstrosity of conflict, came in 1917, when Harry Lauder, a great supporter of wartime charities, released 'Keep Right On To The End Of The Road'. For years, Lauder, whose commercial sentimentality and sending-up of alleged Scottish parsimony often irked his fellow-countrymen, had grown rich on extolling the charms of bonnie lassies and bonnie, bonnie heather. But there was grit and real feeling in 'Keep Right On To The End Of The Road', written after his only son, John, an Argyll and Sutherland Highlanders captain, was killed in action at Pozieres three days after Christmas Day, 1916.

The male impersonator Vesta Tilley was particularly active on the recruiting front, taking on the guise of 'Tommy in the Trench' or 'Jack Tar home from the Sea' to belt out songs such as 'Jolly Good Luck To The Girl Who Loves A Soldier' and 'The Army Of Today's All Right'. The first of these was predictably suggestive:

Don't you think I'm a hero from the wars
Because I'm not,
But nevertheless I've faced powder, don't you see?
I've been in some engagements, too,
And some were deuced hot,
For one of the girls she nearly captured me ...

While the second was simply bumptious in an ironic, jokey way:

So it's all right now,
There's no need to worry any more
I saw the Army wasn't strong,
Everything was wrong
Till the day I came along,
Then the band played, and they all hoorayed.
The Kaiser, they say, went deadly white,
I joined the Army yesterday,
So the Army of today's all right.

These are the kind of numbers that for a while turned Vesta's shows into rallies, prompting some to nickname her 'Britain's best recruiting sergeant'. Sometimes young men were called up on stage to at least declare their intention to join up, and War Bonds were usually on sale. It was the kind of patriotic tub-thumping that deserved a gong – but such were the times, the knighthood in 1919 went not to her but to her impresario husband Walter de Frece, a staunch Conservative supporter and future MP.

Other music-hall songs were more questioning of what it was all about, particularly after 1916 when conscription was introduced. Vesta Tilley herself had one, with 'I've Got A Bit Of A Blighty One':

When they wipe my face with sponges,
And they feed me on blancmanges,
I'm glad I've got a bit of a Blighty one ...

In the same year Florrie Ford and several others were even more explicit in extolling the delights of home – and real home, rather than hospital, in 'Take Me Back To Dear Old Blighty!'; looking back on it today, this can only be seen as an out-and-out anti-war song.

Take me back to dear old Blighty!
Put me on the train for London town!
Take me over there,
Drop me anywhere,
Liverpool, Leeds or Birmingham, well I don't care!

I should love to see my best girl,
Cuddling up again we soon should be,
WHOA!

Tiddley-iddley-ighty,
Hurry me home to Blighty,
Blighty is the place for me!

In 1917 another male impersonator, Ella Shields, pushed the boundaries even further with 'Oh! It's A Lovely War' – 'Who wouldn't be a soldier, eh? Oh, it's a shame to take the pay.' On one level, given these songs' rich seam of irony, it is perhaps surprising that the authorities gave them the nod; or perhaps by then the top brass had recognised that gallows humour, sheer bloody-mindedness – and the beautiful dream of returning home one day – were vital weapons in the average fighting man's armoury.

The Tommies did, of course, have songs of their own, the tunes to some of which might have owed something to the music hall or traditional melodies, but with words forged strictly from the hell of the trenches. 'Bombed Last Night', 'Three German Officers Crossed The Rhine', 'Hanging On The Old Barbed Wire', 'Old Joe Whip', 'Hush, Here Comes A Whizzbang', 'When This Lousy War Is Over', 'I Want To Go Home', 'Far, Far From Wipers', 'I Don't Want To Join The Army', 'We Are Fred Karno's Army' ... These were not what the lads were singing in the trenches at Christmas 1914, however. It was much more likely to be 'Tipperary', 'Home Fires', 'Billy Muggins' – and 'Silent Night'; while music hall was at the heart of their musical world view, Sunday school had made its impact, too.

# 'IT ISN'T WAR, IT'S JUST SLAUGHTER'

With conflict comes censorship, but at the beginning of the First World War it is surprising what escaped the blue pencil, both in terms of press reports and the letters sent back to family and friends from the front and at sea. Ironically, some of the most graphic and horrific accounts were to be found in little local weekly newspapers, the ones routinely dismissed by Fleet Street as the dreary chronicles of weddings, funerals, am dram and vicarage tea parties. What they also had was an intimate relationship with their readers, and if the mayor or local bobby or simply any proud mother or father had had a letter from their son at the front, it was a natural and easy process for it to find its way to the editor's office and from there into the news pages.

The national press was in more of a dilemma, under constant scrutiny by the authorities over its compliance with Section 27 of the Defence of the Realm Act of 1914, in which it was an offence to report anything that might prejudice recruiting or relations with foreign powers, or 'cause disaffection to His Majesty'. It led to a situation in which the government's press bureau and the newspaper barons, notably Northcliffe of *The Times*, *Daily Mail* and *Weekly Despatch*, were forever dancing around one another in their treatment of the topics of the day. Pinning down the exact implication of those Section 27 provisions was a Machiavellian business.

For instance, a report in *The Times* of the debacle of the Mons retreat – 'Our losses are very great. I have seen the broken bits of many regiments' – caused Kitchener apoplexy, yet it emerged that it had been approved by the government's censor, the wily F.E. Smith. 'The British Expeditionary Force has won indeed imperishable glory, but it needs men, men and yet more men,' he had added. 'We want reinforcements and we want them now.' The decision cost Smith his job, yet by the end of the week the cataclysmic report had brought in an unprecedented 175,000 young men clamouring to answer the call to arms. A complex business, news manipulation.

By the time troops were coming home on leave and spreading their version of the truth around their home towns and villages, it became more complex still. Constantly upbeat stories were simply untenable; for many they were simply lies and propaganda, while for those who by chance had not heard factual accounts, they raised impossible hopes of imminent victory, as did claims of German disarray, disaffection and starvation.

That having been said, there was a good deal of self-censorship in the air, particularly among the clutch of illustrated weekly journals that had sprung up to chronicle events within days of the outbreak of hostilities – *T.P.'s Budget*, *The London Illustrated Weekly*, *The War Budget*, *The Penny War Weekly* and the like. So jingoistic were these – portraying the brave Tommies as pure and valiant lions and the Bosch or 'Germ-Huns' as machine-like and ruthless murderers or louche, drunken slobs, depending on the context of the story – that in the end it got in the way of the real story. They encouraged letters from the front, and occasionally let through a tale of some kind of petty fraternisation – opposing troops singing to one another, putting up targets for the others to hit, on one occasion wandering out into no-man's-land to plant a bottle on a stick, dead centre, to see who could hit it first; but when it came to what to us is THE story of that first wartime Christmas, the Christmas Day truce, it so went against the grain of their reportage of the past few months that they could scarcely bring themselves to mention it.

Looking at the troops' letters home, from a distance it is easy to imagine that all that was excised from them was details of troop movements that might have been of value to the enemy, along with anything that might have smacked of mutiny in the ranks. There was certainly no bar on the painful description and denunciation of the war, and while

many letters that found their way into local newspapers could only have upset and demoralised large
numbers of their readers, it seems that little or nothing was done to stop them.

The letter reproduced below was written by Private
A.W. Bick of the First Gloucestershire Regiment after
he had been wounded at Ypres. It had been sent to
his father in Horsley, but was passed on by him to
the local *Stroud News*, which published it two weeks
before Christmas, on 11 December 1914. The newspaper explained that Private Bick had left England
in August, and 'was in the trenches for a month
when he was taken out suffering from fever, which
he contracted after having been fighting with water
up to his waist. He was conveyed to a large hospital
in the north of France, and after remaining there for
a month he returned to the firing line. A few weeks
later he was wounded in the arm, and was treated at
a British Red Cross hospital in a former hotel in Paris,
in the Rue de Presbourg.'

The letter read:

I am now going to try and write a few lines. Note the
address. It is a fine big hotel made into a hospital for the
purpose of soldiers. I am now on my back wounded, but
it is not too serious. It is a slight fracture of a forearm
caused by a bullet. I must thank God it is no worse, for
really I am as lucky a man as there is on this earth. It has
been a regular hell upon earth, and I hope and pray that

it shall please God to bring it to an end soon. It has been a terrible slaughter, and every moment you think it is your turn next, but thank the Lord, he has spared me so far ...

Oh, what terrible sights! I could fill a newspaper with horrors, only I dare not. Never in all my life have I thought about father, mother, sisters and brother like I have this last few months. I think we have about two hundred of our regiment left at the time of writing. G. Moore's brother from Dursley is killed – poor chap. He was only a young fellow. All my chums are either killed or wounded, but at the time of writing, as far as I know, Bill King, Fred Shipton and Bill Maul are alright. Good luck to them!

Oh, how thankful one ought to be to be at home, away from everything. Please remember me to all at home. Remember me next door. I have had to hang on a minute or two as they have been fixing my arm up a bit. It is about twice the usual size. I have had one operation, and I don't know whether or no I have to have another.

It was a week today I received the lead. We were making an attack at Ypres. This is the biggest and bloodiest battle that has ever been fought. It isn't war, it's just slaughter.

# ON CHRISTMAS
# LEAVE

As the poem below was published in *Punch* in December 1916, it is unlikely to have been inspired by anything that might have happened two years earlier; passes back to Blighty little more than four months into the war could not have been expected to have come the way of Tommies like the one evoked here, unless they had suffered some injury that had forced them back to Britain early on and were then lucky enough to have recovered sufficiently to taste Christmas at home before heading back across the Channel.

Nevertheless, the scenario of this poem, mundane as it was, must have been in the dreams, or rather beyond the wildest dreams, of tens of thousands of the boys out there that first Christmas. The poem's author was Wallace Wilfred Blair-Fish, a gentleman journalist and part-time author who lived in part of the Manor House at Blockley in the North Cotswolds, where this story is set. Happily, he survived the war, and was popular around the village

for a few years after it for the short plays he wrote
for the local amateur dramatic society. While of
officer class, he slipped into the role of a humble
private with affection and ease for the purpose of
'On Christmas Leave'.

Blockley, then in Worcestershire but part of
Gloucestershire since 1931, is seen by its admir-
ers as one of the most beautiful villages in the
Cotswolds, with buildings of strikingly rich golden
stone. In the eighteenth century it was a centre for
water-powered textile mills and far later than that,
by the mid-1880s, six mills provided work for about
600 people preparing silk for the ribbon-making
factories of Coventry. That industry had all but
died away by the time Blair-Fish was living there,
and the village he knew was a beautiful, remote
rural spot in terminal decline as an industrial
centre. Today, the then near-derelict mills along the
Blockley Brook have been transformed into some of
the most desirable homes in the Cotswolds.

Among the poem's personnel, Chainey, the landlord of the Crown, did indeed run a horse-drawn
bus to the Great Western Railway station, which
was 1.5 miles or more from the village and would
have acquired the GWR's notorious 'Road' suffix –
Tetbury Road, Clarbeston Road – had it been much
further away from the community it purported
to serve. On the Paddington line to Worcester
and Hereford, the station closed as a result of the

To be home on leave that first Christmas was almost
exclusively the preserve of the injured. The officer seen here,
with his 'shrapnel-injured arm', seems to be faring better
than most in this illustration from the *Penny War Weekly*'s
Boxing Day number. (*Penny War Weekly*, 26 December 1914)

Beeching cuts in the early 1960s, a fate which also befell the poetically more famous Adlestrop not many miles up the line. The retired military man was Major Spencer, at that time land agent for the neighbouring Northwick Park estate; and as Westmacott's Mill is the largest of the village's former textile factories, we can only assume that the old chap shuffling around with the collecting plate was a member of that prominent local family. The Twelve Apostles, presumably one of a string of pubs to cater for the mill workers, has long since ceased trading.

Blair-Fish's poem is not to be found in any of the great anthologies of First World War poetry, but those comparatively few who know it feel it rings true where the works of many more celebrated poets of the conflict sound a false note. If nothing else, it gives us an insight into the tranquil, deeply rural background from which so many young men emerged to face the unspeakable chaos of war.

> When I got into Chainey's bus
> Down at the station it began,
> I didn't feel a fighting man
> No more: the old hills made no fuss
> at seeing me; the winding road
> That troops and transports never knowed,
> And the old station nag's click-clack
> Just took me back.

The Twelve Apostles' boughs were bare
Just as they was last time I came.
Mother was looking just the same
And father hadn't turned a hair.
I washed as usual at the pump;
My bed had got the same old lump;
Dick lived next door – I near forgot
I seen him shot.

Church wasn't changed on Christmas Day –
Old Westmacott took round the plate;
The old Major stood up stiff and straight
And it seemed somehow just like play
Salutin' him, retired an' all.
Home – No, the war, I think – seems small.
This evening I go back to France
And take my chance.

# SHOT
## AT DAWN

Christmas 1914 was the time the game was up for Joe
Ball and Fred Sheffield, who slipped away from the
ranks of the Middlesex Regiment's Second Battalion
and tried hopelessly and in vain to merge into
French civilian life. Their dream, like that of most
deserters, must have been somehow to find their way
to the coast and befriend a willing fisherman who
would carry them back home across that tantalis-
ingly narrow stretch of water. Today we would say
'Dream on'. Back then, the lads in the trenches would
have shrugged and muttered 'Some hopes'.

They were discovered in a barn no great distance
from where they had gone missing, protesting
they were French but knowing they were doomed.
Perhaps they had been unaware the farmer had spot-
ted them; perhaps they had made themselves known
to him and he had shown them to the barn before
alerting the authorities, fearing the worst if he had
been discovered sheltering deserters. Whatever the

story, Ball and Sheffield were hustled back to their unit, tried on 30 December and shot at dawn on 12 January in the first double execution of the war. Coincidentally, the following day, an order was issued which reversed the concept of presumed innocence. From then on, the likes of Joe and Fred would be deemed guilty unless they could provide compelling evidence to the contrary. For these two, however, it mattered not; under either system, they were dead men as soon as their pursuers burst into that barn.

As is well known, deserters suffering from shell shock and complete mental breakdown were shown no mercy by the ad hoc military courts, so Ball and Sheffield stood no chance. They were not among their battalion's old sweats who had fought in the Boer War, but nevertheless, they were regular soldiers who had joined the regiment in the summer of 1912, when jobs were scarce, and had undergone thorough training before sailing for France in the weeks after war had been declared. Their battalion was heading for the front when they took flight, an advance that would culminate in the bloody Battle of Neuve Chapelle three months later. We can only surmise that Privates Ball, a 20-year-old from Queen's Park, and Sheffield, who was 26 and from Tottenham, had heard on the grapevine of the horrors of Mons and the Marne and decided that this was not what they had joined the army for.

Most deserters were tried and executed within twenty-four hours, but with their battalion on the march, Joe and Fred were kept waiting a full two weeks before they faced a firing squad of their colleagues; a wretched time, but there were probably odd acts of kindness from old mates detailed to guard them, the quick drag on a shared fag or a laugh about old times. In some cases, enlightened officers and chaplains would tell the condemned that what they did was not a capital offence in itself, but the punishment was necessary to deter others from doing the same – so in dying they, too, were in a way giving their lives for their country's cause. The effect of such words surely differed from one man to another – and in the case of Ball and Sheffield, on the run before a bullet had been fired anywhere near them, it is doubtful whether they would ever have been uttered at all. The pair would have had a priest with them in their final hours, however, and if their senses were dulled with morphine or rum, they would not have been the first or last.

It was a chaplain named Julian Bickersteth's unpleasant lot to find himself detailed to sit through the night with one such condemned man, in a room only some 9 feet by 10 feet and with two guards also present. The prisoner did not want to know about the priest's attempts to comfort him with prayers or readings, but insisted that the two of them should sing hymns together – which they did for some three hours, and never the same one twice. In a letter home to his family, Canon Bickersteth wrote: 'He said "We haven't finished yet; we must have 'God Save The King'".

And then and there we rose to our feet and the two Military Police ... had to get up and stand rigidly to attention while the prisoner and I sang lustily three verses of the National Anthem ... I have never spent a stranger evening.'

The (at that time) unique double execution would have called for extra planning, with two squads of six men mustered and an officer and the chaplain in attendance. A medical officer would have placed pieces of white cloth over the blindfolded Ball and Sheffield's hearts; and as was routine, their comrades detailed to perform the miserable task of dispatching them would be told that one of the six rifles was loaded with a blank, so that each could take comfort in the thought that maybe he had not fired a fatal shot. Bound to stakes, the fallen men would then have been examined by the medic, and if either had by chance survived the officer would have finished him off with a revolver.

No written account of Joe and Fred's execution exists, but a report by a French military observer of his nation's mode of operation, published on the excellent History Learning Site, paints a macabre picture:

> The two condemned were tied up from head to toe like sausages. A thick bandage hid their faces. And, a horrible thing, on their chests a square of fabric was placed over their hearts. The unfortunate duo could not move. They had to be carried like two dummies on the open-backed lorry, which bore them to the rifle range. It is

impossible to articulate the sinister impression the sight
of those two living parcels made on me.

The padre mumbled some words and then went off to
eat. Two six-strong platoons appeared, lined up with their
backs to the firing posts. The guns lay on the ground.
When the condemned had been attached, the men of the
platoon, who had not been able to see events, respond-
ing to a silent gesture, picked up their guns, abruptly
turned about, aimed and opened fire. Then they turned
their backs on the bodies and the sergeant ordered
'Quick march!' The men marched right past them, without inspecting their weapons, without turning a head.
No military compliments, no parade, no music, no march
past; a hideous death without drums or trumpets.

The image of the condemned man as a near-lifeless
package before he is shot was repeated in Commander
Frank Percy Crozier's book *A Brass Hat In No Man's
Land*, in which he looked back on an execution in 1916.
He named the soldier Crocker, though nobody of anything like that name appears in the records of those
shot at dawn. (There is, ironically, a Rifleman Crozier):

As for Crocker, he leaves this earth, in so far as knowing
anything of his surroundings is concerned, by midnight,
for I arrange that enough spirituous liquor is left beside
him to sink a ship ... The victim is carried to the stake.
He is far too drunk to walk ... As he is produced I see that
he is practically lifeless and quite unconscious. He has

already been bound with ropes. There are hooks on the post ... He is hooked on like dead meat at a butcher's shop. His eyes are bandaged – not that it really matters, for he is already blind.

It must be added that not every senior officer took such thorough steps to anaesthetise the condemned.

Men were tried without legal representation by three officers; the option of a 'prisoner friend' to bear witness for them was often forfeited as a futile gesture, and while legally, every court martial should have had a 'judge advocate' present, very few did at or close to the front. Condemned men, on the night before their execution, had the right to petition the King for clemency, but the fact that not a single one ever made that last desperate plea for life suggests universal ignorance of the rule. Again, it would have been to no avail, but it might have brought an extra day on earth and one last flicker of hope, and it is hard to imagine that not a single soul would have gone for it, given the chance.

The government's tacit acceptance that these were desperate measures for a desperate situation is borne out by the fact that not a single man who went missing from his unit on British soil faced the firing squad – an explanation, maybe, of the fact that four times as many men deserted in the United Kingdom than in France and Belgium.

On 18 December, at much the time Joe and Fred were on the run in France, the *Stroud News* carried a report of the appearance before the town's magistrates' court of George Couldray and Arthur Winstone of Chalford, who had gone missing from the Third Battalion, the Gloucestershire Regiment's base at Woolwich Barracks a few days earlier. In ordering them back to their unit under escort, the chairman, a solicitor, said 'he could not understand fine looking young fellows like the prisoners deserting from the service just when their country most needed them. He hoped that when they returned to their regiment they would atone for what they had done by good conduct.'

Not death at dawn, then, but a wigging from the local beak; and though the terms of their atonement might well have been tough, they did not compare with the price paid by Joe and Fred – or the scores of poor wretches who walked away from the action racked by shell shock or insanity through the undreamed-of horrors they had witnessed. It also appears that George Couldray and Arthur Winstone survived the fighting, since their names do not appear on Chalford's war memorial, while those of the doubtless related Fred Couldray and William Winstone do.

The hole-and-corner nature of military executions is reflected by the fact that neither Joe Ball nor Fred Sheffield, who could hardly have died in more controlled or formal circumstances, has a known grave. Both, however – in among the other fallen members of their battalion and regiment but coldly labelled 'Shot at Dawn' – appear on the extensive war memorial in

Le Touret Military Cemetery at Richebourg-l'Avoue.
This records the 13,000-plus men of Britain and the
empire who fell in this area between the beginning
of the war and September 1915, and whose remains
are untraced.

They are also among the total of 306 men executed
by British firing squads in the First World War – among
them twenty-five Canadians, twenty-two Irishmen
and five New Zealanders – who are commemorated
at the Shot at Dawn memorial which was unveiled at
the National Memorial Arboretum in Staffordshire in
2001. The memorial was a milestone along the way
for campaigners whose aims were finally achieved
when the government issued a mass pardon for all
306 in November 2006, and on the hundredth anniversary of the outbreak of war in August 2014 the
Ecumenical Society for Peace held a candle-lit vigil in
which the names of Joe, Fred and the other 304 were
read out. The 306 candles were lit at sunset and then
the group 'watched and waited with them, remember-
ing their final hours' until sunrise, when the flames
were extinguished. A scripture verse, poem or medita-
tion was read on the stroke of every hour.

The military death penalty was abolished in 1930,
an influential campaigner against it being Ernest
Thurtle, a wounded soldier who became Labour MP
for Shoreditch in 1923. He first introduced a Bill in
1924 and abolition became Labour policy a year later,
but Lords opposition meant that it was another five

years before it was carried. Lawrence of Arabia was a prominent supporter, but various retired generals including Lord Allenby led bitter opposition, arguing that threat of capital punishment stiffened the resolve of the men. That argument was countered by the fact that the Australians had joined the war effort on the strict understanding that none of their men would be executed for cowardice or desertion, yet their troops had clearly been at least as effective as any others.

A more potent impact was made on public opinion by Thurtle's pamphlet *Shootings At Dawn: The Army Death Penalty At Work*. Drawing on anguished letters written to him by troops who had witnessed executions or been hapless members of firing squads, it threw light on a murky corner of the war's history that the authorities would have far preferred to have consigned to obscurity.

Today, the ritualised killing of seriously ill and often extremely young servicemen – some no more than 15 when they lied their way into the army to serve their country – is universally seen as obscene. Yet it is possible to begin to understand how the circumstances arose; the top brass had enough on their hands with the enemy to spend too much time worrying about the niceties of natural justice in an arena in which suddenly the price of a young man's life was bewilderingly and disorientingly low. Joe Ball and Fred Sheffield simply took their chance, as tens of thousands of their fellow troops were doing every day; it did not pay off for them, but they were far from alone in that.

# DOVER,
# FIRST AND LAST

In the early days of the war the threat from the air had
been more imagined than real, with deadly Zeppelins
emerging from the mist and wreaking havoc widely
seen as a more potent menace than anything an aeroplane might do. After all, it was just eleven years since
the Wright brothers first coaxed a powered aircraft over
800 or so feet in fifty-nine seconds before crash-landing,
and most flying machines still looked like glorified kites.
Zeppelins, on the other hand – substantial, menacing-
looking, hundreds of feet long – had given the Germans
dominance in the sky for twenty years.

Yet the earliest bomb to be dropped on English soil
was from an aircraft. True, the first Zeppelin weighed in
early in the new year, killing twenty and injuring forty
in unsuspecting Great Yarmouth and King's Lynn; but
the first explosive from the air fell on Dover at around
a quarter to eleven in the morning on Christmas Eve,
1914. The pilot, who had apparently crossed the
Channel alone from the burgeoning German airbase

at Zeebrugge, was Oberleutnant-zur-See Stephan von Prondzynski, who at what he took to be the operative moment, at a height of 5,000 feet, reached down, lifted the bomb from the floor of his cockpit and held it steadily over the side before letting go, with Dover Castle as his target. It would have been a significant hit, symbolically, at least – a medieval stronghold against invaders that had been massively strengthened many times since the Middle Ages, not least during the Napoleonic Wars. But instead he (perhaps not surprisingly) got his timing wrong and missed by some 400 yards inland to the north west; the bomb landed in magistrate Thomas Terson's kitchen garden at the end of Leyburne Road, made a wide hole, broke windows up to 200 yards away, and in the garden of St James' Rectory next door, blew Mr James Banks off a ladder from which he had been collecting holly to decorate the church. He was no more than bruised, despite falling some 20 feet, but although damage caused by the raid totalled an irksome but far from devastating £40, the raid gave Dover and the rest of the country plenty to think about. Two aircraft scrambled to see Prondzynski off, and off he went, unscathed.

If the pilot had happened to hit St James' church, the outrage it would have caused, eight days after the Germans' 'baby-killing' bombardment of the north east, can only be imagined. It was fashionable to paint the foe as barbarian and unholy, the ones who did not have God on their side. As it was, the church survived enemy bombing in both world wars, only to be declared redundant and demolished after much of its parish had been reduced to rubble in the 1939–45 conflict. The earlier St James' church it had succeeded was very badly damaged by shell fire, but fragments of it, including a Norman arch, have been made good and survive as a war memorial.

The Press Association's local correspondent had a lively day. 'While the townspeople of Dover were busy with their Christmas trade on Thursday morning, they were startled at about 10.45 by a terrible explosion, the concussion being felt throughout the town,' he wrote, before continuing:

> It was found to have been caused by a bomb dropped over the town by a German, fortunately with the result only of shattering glass windows and no loss of life. The enemy airman came from the direction of Deal, and passing over Dover Castle, shot out of a cloud and dropped his bomb. If he intended it for the Castle, the airman was wide of his mark, as the missile fell into a garden owned by Mr T.A. Terson J.P. at the rear of St James' Rectory. It exploded with terrible force and made a hole in the ground about three feet in depth and eight to ten feet in width.
>
> Earth was thrown in all directions, some falling into the roadway twenty yards away. Houses within a radius of two hundred yards had their windows shattered, and the foundations of these buildings were shaken. A large piece of shell was found on the verandah of a

house in Victoria Park, two hundred yards distant, and in Maison Dieu Road several houses had their windows broken. At St James' Rectory the rector and his family happened to be out, but the cook was struck by some falling glass. Luckily, she was not injured. A man working at the rectory was cutting greenery from a tree for church decoration, and the force of the explosion hurled him to the ground, a distance of nearly twenty feet. The force of his fall, fortunately, was broken, and he was uninjured.

Only a few persons actually saw the bomb descending. Mr Mowll, son of a member of Messrs Mowll and Mowll, the well-known Kentish solicitors, stated that he was in the roadway talking to a friend when he heard a screeching sound, and looking up, saw the bomb during the last two hundred yards of its fall. It left a trail of smoke in its wake, and some flying earth struck him. Only one explosion took place, so that apparently only one bomb was fired, the airman then beating a hurried retreat.

Aeroplanes and seaplanes were on the wing at once, but the German machine, travelling at such a great height, had the advantage, and quickly crossed the Channel in a south-easterly direction, making for the Belgian coast. Although naturally excited by the explosion, which caused crowds to rush to the sea front, the townspeople remained very calm, and by mid-day the business of the town was proceeding just as usual.

There had been a prior warning of the unwelcome visit three days earlier, on 21 December, when an

Albatros BII-W seaplane or floatplane designed by a young Ernst Heinkel dropped two 20-pound fragment bombs unchallenged into the sea some 400 yards south west of Admiralty Pier, again in broad daylight, at one o'clock in the afternoon. The Zeebrugge pilots were apparently vying to see who would be the first to drop a bomb on British soil, and as events turned out, it was not surprising that Prondzynski was the daredevil who was prepared to fly that extra few hundred yards over English soil, while his colleague had thought better of it. Twenty-four hours later, on Christmas Day, he launched the first bombing raid on London Docks and the Medway, for which he and his observer were awarded the Iron Cross, while in February 1915 he pushed the boundaries again when he and his crewman passed over Clacton, flew inland 25 miles to Braintree, where they dropped two incendiary bombs, and then dropped further explosives on Coggeshall and Colchester Barracks before heading for home. Again, little damage was done – but if Braintree was within range, where else might be?

Five days later Prondzynski's was one of three seaplanes that set out once more for Britain, but this time fortune was against him. It was probably engine trouble that brought his aircraft down in the North Sea on a desperately cold and blustery evening, and he and his colleague were happy to be picked up by a British tug and taken as prisoners to Lowestoft after clinging to wreckage through a night of high seas and snowstorms.

Early reports were that the aircraft that dropped that first bomb on English soil was a Taube built by the Rumpler company, but it is now accepted that it was the same Friedrichshafen FF29 that bombed London Docks the following day. A seaplane that had entered service with the German Imperial Navy only the previous month, it was a monoplane like the better-known Taube – the 'Dove' – which had been first developed in 1909 from original glider designs, and was by this time imperial Germany's first viable military aircraft, mass-produced by dozens of companies licensed to assemble it. The FF29 had followed on, but soon proved as unequal to modern warfare as the Taube.

As the war progressed, Dover suffered many more air raids; given its location, that was hardly surprising, but it is surely coincidental that having fallen victim to Britain's first aerial bombing, on Christmas Eve 1914, it also suffered its last. That was on Whit Sunday night, 19 and 20 May 1918, and though the four bombs dropped were some of the heaviest the town had suffered, the outcome in terms of casualties was precisely as it had been that first Christmas – one person slightly injured, this time a Miss Joad. The difference, however, was that damage to property was quite considerable, even though one of the bombs failed to explode; and by now, though the bomber breached the home defences, getting away scot-free had become a more demanding task. The offending aircraft was brought down into the sea and at around midnight a long salvo from the gun battery accounted for another, one of the frightening Siemens-Schuckert R.VIIIs, a five-engined giant of the kind that looked like something out of a nightmare and would indeed have been undreamed-of when the war began. Finally, at around twenty to one in the morning, six more bombs fell at St Margaret's and a further six dropped on Swingate Aerodrome (causing no damage). These were the last to rain down on England; for a little over twenty years, anyway.

A curious postscript: a few years later, in the 1920s, the map and guidebook publishers Ward, Lock & Co. updated their guide to Dover, St Margaret's Bay and Deal for a post-war audience. 'By reason of its geographical position and its possession of a spacious harbour, Dover's experiences during the Great War were unique,' it reported. 'For residents there were the thrilling experiences of attacks by Zeppelins, seaplanes, aeroplanes, destroyers and submarines. In all, Dover had one hundred and thirteen warnings.' It is hard to believe that 'thrilling' was quite the way the townsfolk would have described their experiences at the time; particularly on Christmas Eve 1914, when a raid that in reality achieved very little seemed to pose such a potent threat to the well-being of the whole of southern England.

# THE POPE'S
# FAILED BID
# FOR A CEASEFIRE

As we know, there were ad hoc lulls in fighting along both the Western and Eastern Fronts at Christmas 1914, but a bid by the recently elected Pope Benedict XV to broker a more formal and, he hoped, lasting settlement came to nothing. It was hardly surprising. Of the warring nations, only France was predominantly Roman Catholic, while as a known pacifist, his was a voice in the wilderness at a time when belligerent attitudes were hardening on all sides by the day.

The white smoke had scarcely cleared from the roof of the Vatican before the former Cardinal Giacomo della Chiesa was faced with shaping his church's attitude towards the war. An intellectual and skilled diplomat from a wealthy family, he quickly decided that neutrality, the easing of suffering and the promotion of peace were to be the keynotes of his reign, and long before the handshakes in no-man's-land he had made a Christmas truce his first substantial objective. Roman Catholic a great deal of Northern Europe was not, but nevertheless, he was far from alone in shrinking from the concept of man killing fellow man on the Lord's birthday, as the spontaneous Christmas Day fraternisation made plain; nevertheless, a formal ceasefire that might lead to a more lasting settlement of accounts? That was never on the agenda for either side.

It was easy to put the proposals on the back burner, as the Vatican was forced reluctantly to accept. The Western churches' Christmas Day was different from the Orthodox Russians', and besides, the latter set greater store by Easter as a feast day. For the Germans' ally Turkey and the Allies' Japan, Christmas meant nothing, anyway. The hope of a single day when peace ruled on earth, however uneasily, was doomed from the start.

Grassroots reaction at home varied widely, but the editor of a small newspaper in southern England probably summed up the attitude the authorities would have wished the nation to take when he wrote in his 25 December issue:

> The Papal proposal that a Christmas truce be observed between the combatants has not found acceptance, although we are given by Germany to understand that both she and Austria were in favour of it. Turkey, too, with whom Christmas is an infidel institution, gave her cordial assent to the Pope's proposal! But the Allies had good cause to be sceptical of the Germo-Austro-Turko combination's good faith in truces, and we think they did the right thing in not encouraging the idea.

From what we know of Germany, she would have spent the time allowed for the truce in planning a surprise attack and taking advantage of her enemies' good faith in every conceivable way, and her wiles would have been cheerfully seconded by the crafty Turk. With enemies that systematically murder non-combatants and innocent women and children, that violate every pledge to serve their ends, that disregard every convention to which they have put their signature, no truce can be arranged until they put down their arms and surrender unconditionally.

For our brave sailors and soldiers, a few days' respite from the horrors of war would have been the most welcome gift the Government could have given them during this Christmastide, but if the respite were attended by the constant fear of treachery on the part of their foes, our men would infinitely prefer to do without it.

So wrote an armchair general from Stroud, Gloucestershire, and no doubt the majority of real-life British generals would have echoed his words. Today, the concept of the slippery Germans and their cohorts using the day to regroup and plan their next move, while the British top brass presumably devoted the respite entirely to plum duff and candied fruits, seems somewhat bizarre; and here, too, is a familiar sighting of our old friend 'the crafty Turk', a character who would inhabit the imaginings of elderly men well into the second half of the last century, along

with the 'Yellow Peril' and the inadvisability of playing cards with Greeks.

Benedict XV's brief pontificate – he fell ill with
pneumonia and died in January 1922 – saw him
continue to strive against the Great War, which he
saw as 'useless slaughter' and 'the suicide of Europe'.
He put in place significant humanitarian projects,
including a Vatican bureau which genuinely helped
prisoners of war, refugees, deportees, the wounded
and the persecuted from all sides, regardless of their
political or religious beliefs, but his repeated efforts
to negotiate peace came to nothing. His seven-point
peace proposal of August 1917, demanding an
immediate ceasefire, a lowering of armament stocks,
guaranteed safety on the seas and international arbi-
tration was ignored entirely by the European powers,
while the United States President, Woodrow Wilson,
dismissed any declaration of peace as premature.
In Europe, each side saw Benedict as biased towards
the other, which would prompt some to argue today
that this was a sign that he was on the right track;
but the real indication that his efforts were seen as
an irrelevance came with the Paris peace conference
of 1919, when there was no place for the Vatican at
the table at Versailles. What was seen as his weak-
ness, even among some of his fellow countrymen
in Italy, was his unwavering, deep-seated pacifism;
after all, what place was there for a pacifist at a
peace conference?

Instead, he wrote an encyclical pleading for international reconciliation, *Pacem, Dei Munus Pulcherrimum* (*On Peace and Christian Reconciliation*). It is little-read today, but his efforts for world peace during his turbulent reign have not been forgotten in other ways. In St Peter's Cathedral in Rome a statue shows him at prayer, kneeling above a tomb decorated with olive branches, that symbolises the graves throughout Europe that commemorate those who fell in battle and the innocent victims of the war. Above the statue is the Virgin Mary presenting the infant Jesus, the Prince of Peace, to a world in flames.

The monument, by Pietro Canonica, a renowned Italian sculptor whose work includes a bust of Edward VII in Buckingham Palace, was unveiled in 1928; but another statue of Benedict was completed in his lifetime, in 1921, and that still stands in the unlikely city of Istanbul. Admittedly, it is in the courtyard of the Cathedral of the Holy Spirit, but members of the Muslim majority in the city played their full part in placing it there; the Pope helped establish a hospital on the Syrian border where injured Turkish soldiers were treated, and Sultan Mehmet VI is believed to have been a grateful and willing subscriber to his statue.

Showing a troubled-looking Benedict giving his blessing to the world, its inscription describes him as 'The great Pope of the world tragedy ... the benefactor of all people, irrespective of nationality or religion'.

It has been visited by several popes over the years, including Paul VI, John Paul II – and Benedict XVI, for whose visit in 2006 it was spruced up by the city council. The name of the latter, let it be noted, is not coincidental; when Cardinal Joseph Ratzinger became pope in 2005, he took on his papal name in specific tribute to Benedict XV for his untiring quest for peace in the First World War – a quest that began, passionately but sadly unsuccessfully, at Christmas 1914.

# FUNNY
## OLD FRITZ

A one-off, once-in-a-wartime phenomenon – that is
what is said so often of the Christmas truce of 1914,
and so it was, in its intensity, scope and impact on
society; but when it came to fraternisation it was
not the beginning or end of the story, not by a long
way. Troops writing home were forever regaling their
families with stories of what funny old Fritz was up
to on the other side of the wires. For a start, it was
a more pleasant aspect of life to share with the folks
than a lot that was going on. Besides which, in the
quiet times, in the times when the top brass on both
sides accepted it was a stalemate along their stretch
of the front until they or the other lot came up with
something different, there really was not a great deal
to do other than make yourself as dry and clean and
comfortable and well fed as you could, spend time
with the workmates whose company you enjoyed
most and keep a weather eye on what the neighbours
in the other trench were up to. Dirt and danger were

facts of life in the trenches, but in-between-times it could be a boring old existence for a fit and active young man.

It tended to be when trenches were as close together as 60 yards or less that the interaction set in; half the length of a football pitch, from goal-line to centre spot. There are records of their being as close as 13 yards – a small suburban garden from house wall to back fence, less than two-thirds of a cricket pitch – and that really was a ridiculous situation, one neither side wanted but which had come about in that haphazard, chaotic way that absurdities do come about in war. When the newspapers were first reporting trench warfare in the autumn of 1914 it sounded almost laughable to some at home, two lines of men eyeing one another through peepholes in parapets; by the time you were 13 yards apart, the alternative to laughable could only be tragic.

Even at three times that distance, the other side was always with you. You could hear snatches of conversation over there, the clatter of washing up, songs or shouts if the chaps were having a particularly animated game of cards or if the mail wagon had called with letters from wives and girlfriends. There would be familiar voices: the boomer, little squeaky, laughing boy, nasty cough, the nightingale. However outlandish their names might have appeared in the army ledgers, by the time they were yelling at one another along the line, you soon realised that Willi, Wolfi, Albi, Siggi and the rest might well have been your mates in the factory back home in another life. At some points it got to lobbing gifts one to the other, tobacco or sausages, weighed down with clods of earth.

There were in-jokes. From the late nineteenth century hundreds of thousands of families had left Germany as economic migrants – not persecuted minorities, but simply people in search of a better life. As a New World promised a new life, large numbers of them crossed the Atlantic for America; but a significant minority had settled for Britain, meaning that throughout the German Army were men who had worked in London, Manchester, Glasgow, Cardiff and many other major cities, as waiters, barbers, pork butchers and musicians among various other service occupations.

Hear the little German band,
Da, da, da, da, da, da, da,
Just let me hold your hand dear ...

Florrie Forde had sung in the halls, and it was no surprise to our troops that there was sometimes a decent oom-pah band not far behind the enemy trenches. It was for their work in catering, however, that the Germans were best known: 'Shout "Waiter!" and you'll see a dozen heads pop up from behind that parapet!' This was also the explanation why, as is forever the case in dialogue between the British and foreigners, it is the latter who have the verbal glue to stick the conversation together. The Jerry who talked Cockney, the Yank Jerry, the Scotch Jerry: along the opposition line you would hear English spoken in all manner of surprising accents.

Apart from the banter and occasional lobbed gifts, snippets of genuinely useful information might be exchanged. When Saxon conscripts were about to be replaced by fierce and battle-hardened Prussians, they would warn the other side that things might hot up a bit next week. One Tommy wrote home and said that when one of his mates decided he had had enough of this tomfoolery and started abusing the Germans and calling them square-heads and so on, 'they just laughed'. The angry man's less belligerent colleagues were more of the view that they had picked up on the rhythm of life on the other side, recognised that it was not so different from their own, and fretted if it sounded more pleasant and exciting than what they were going through. There was a deepening feeling that both sides were in the same line of business; although at opposite ends of the shop floor, they were interdependent one upon the other. What they did, you did. Why upset the applecart?

As Christmas 1914 approached the British top brass were growing increasingly uneasy about what they saw happening. Early in December an order went out expressly forbidding fraternisation, 'for it discourages initiative in commanders and destroys the offensive spirit in all ranks ... Friendly intercourse with the enemy, unofficial armistices and the exchange of tobacco and other comforts ... are absolutely prohibited.' The widespread grassroots dismissal of this directive at Christmas, up to at least junior officer level, tells us precisely how serious a disciplinary issue this had become – and why, twelve months on, the generals made strenuous and successful steps to ensure it would not happen again.

Beyond mere words, commanders at the front decided the deadlock had to be broken by swift and

German bands were familiar to Tommies both before the war and during it, when live music would sometimes drift across from enemy positions. This group, in a barracks behind the trenches, consists of wine bottle chimes, mandolin, side drum, accordion, triangle, tin whistle and an oriental-looking stringed instrument, possibly home-made. (*The Illustrated War News*, 20 January 1915)

aggressive action, raids on entrenched German positions that would dispel all thoughts of live and let live. All were disastrous for the British forces – at Wytschaete on 4 December, twice at La Boutillerie on the 18th and most wasteful of life of all, at Ploegsteert Wood the following day. All it told the Tommies, and indeed many of their leaders in the thick of it, was that it was not without reason that the two forces had sat looking one another in the face for weeks on end. If Plugstreet was the solution to deadlock, it was not a very good one, was it?

Many letters telling of odd incidents between the lines found their way into the weekly war magazines that had sprung up within days or weeks of the start of the conflict. Every last one of these periodicals was staunchly jingoistic, and it is to their credit that they published these testimonies from the front, since in spirit they ran diametrically counter to their editorial line. Usually the stories would be printed without comment, though sometimes the point would be made that Tommy was a forgiving and good-natured soul, in contrast to the cold-hearted and treacherous foe. On the evidence of these letters, this was far from Tommy's experience of 'our friend the enemy' Fritz.

Today, it could be argued that there is more verbally violent animosity between supporters of small local rival football teams – Exeter and Torquay, say, Bury and Rochdale, Swindon and Oxford – than there is expressed in these long-ago dispatches from the trenches; and that was the way it stayed in many parts of the front until well into 1916, when each side was so traumatised by the horror of it all that nothing other than grim survival mattered any more.

There follow extracts from letters that found their way into various publications, while the later final reminiscence is to be found in *Somme Harvest: Memories of a PBI in the summer of 1916*, by Giles E.M. Eyre:

> The German soldier is not the down-hearted kind of man that everybody tries to believe. Night upon night we hear them singing their patriotic Kaiser Bill kind of songs in their trenches, and they even join in the chorus of that 'Tipperary' thing ... which, I think, shows they are not as blue [sad] as people like to believe. They have also got a brass band somewhere behind their trenches, which sometimes plays in the evening.

English Officer, *T.P.'s Journal Of Great Deeds Of The Great War*, 19 December 1914:

> Last night the enemy sang in the trenches and cheered. They ended up with 'God Save The King', in English. They were trying to drag us on and think they were drunk again, but we sang 'Billy Muggins' to 'em. We frequently give our friends the enemy a song in the trenches at night, and it seems funny to hear two rival armies singing the same hymn.

Lance-Corporal Winpenny, Royal Berkshire Regiment, *Penny War Weekly*, 2 January 1915:

We are very friendly with the Germans in some parts of the line. In one place they have been putting bottles on the parapets of the trenches to see who could knock them down first. First we would put a bottle on our trench, and then they would put one on theirs. After a bit they agreed to have a bottle in the middle, and a German stalked out and put a bottle on a stick in between. However, just then, a six-inch shell got into the German trenches, so the match was stopped. Since then friendly relations have been opened again, and our fellows are swapping bits of bread for eagles off German helmets! I expect you will think I got this out of *Punch* or something, but it is quite true.

Officer, Royal Engineers, *T.P.'s Journal Of Great Deeds Of The Great War*, 2 January 1915:

The amenities of trench life are somewhat humorous occasionally. In places we are so near to the enemy that the men can shout across to each other, and the Germans even mark our shots, sometimes, as if we were shooting at a rifle range. For instance, the other day in one trench they would keep on indicating misses as the shots were fired, and occasionally they would signal a bull's eye when we hit anyone. In two cases the Cornwalls saw Germans fall hit when the bull's eye was signalled.

Brigadier, Royal Engineers, *T.P.'s Journal Of Great Deeds Of The Great War*, 2 January 1915:

The Germans are a comical lot, very amusing some-times. Their trenches are very near to ours, in some places about sixty yards apart, so you can guess that we can see pretty well what they do, and hear what they say. Only the other morning they stuck up a board with these words chalked on it: 'Are you Englishmen?' We promptly replied: 'No, we are noblemen.' It's very amus-ing to hear them mocking us in English. If we fire a shot amiss up comes a red flag; or if it happened to be a near one, they signal the shots up with a spade, the same as they do on the ranges.

Lance-Corporal S. Lookin, Second Scottish Rifles, *Penny Vivid War Weekly*, 21 January 1915:

A voice with a marked Yankee twang hailed us from the Hun sap ... 'I guess you yobs have some corned beef, biscuits and jam to spare there, hein?' 'We might,' answered Marriner. 'What will you give us for them?' 'Some cigars, Schnapps, and Johan here will play you tunes on his violin. If you take it easy today, we do the same. You don't bomb, we don't bomb, that right, eh?' 'All right, Yank, chuck us over your cigars and the Schnapps, whatever it is, and over comes some bully and jam ...' We looked up as three or four bundles came sailing over and fell in and on the sap edge. 'Duck your nuts, boys,' urged Oldham cautiously. 'Old Fritz may have something up his sleeve.' However, nothing untoward happened. We retrieved the bundles. Fat cigars and a couple of soda-water bottles filled with yellowish spirit. 'All A1, old cock,' replied Marriner cheerfully. 'Here comes our whack,' and over we slung sundry tins of jam, bully, Maconochie [tinned beef and vegetable stew] and packets of Army biscuits. Quiet reigned over all. 'Now this is what I call a bit of all right,' purred Marriner contentedly as he squatted down, drawing at a cigar and occasionally having a swig of Schnapps.

Second Lieutenant Giles Eyre, King's Royal Rifle Corps, *Somme Harvest: Memories of a PBI in the summer of 1916.*

# THE TRUCE
# TO END
# ALL TRUCES

There were two phenomena of the early months of the First World War that were seized upon by people who longed to detect some sort of higher purpose beyond the clamour and stench and squalor of the industrial-scale death and destruction at the front. One was the apparently widespread sighting of the Angels of Mons after the battle of that name in August, with the war no more than weeks old; and the other was the Christmas Truce, when for a brief spell an uneasy peace descended on some of those whose unhappy lot it was to find themselves at the sharpest of sharp ends in the killing fields.

There was a difference between these two stories which is all too obvious to us now but which at the time seemed to escape the grasp of a large number of intelligent and rational people, and it was this: one was a fairy story pure and simple, the other a true story made all the more remote and ethereal by the certain knowledge that it would never happen again.

The myth was the story of the Angels of Mons, a heavenly host of what to some people looked more like Agincourt longbowmen than winged beings, who moved across the skies to watch over the exhausted British troops as they retreated in the face of overwhelming opposition. The London press put spin on this enforced military withdrawal in a variety of ways, with the greater or lesser approval of the War Office: one was that it was a tactical pulling back, rather than a rout, which (in that the British Expeditionary Force quite quickly regrouped and advanced again) it technically was; another was that it proved the pressing need for more fighting men, and young civilians promptly answered the call to arms in their hundreds of thousands; and then, revealed months after the event, there was this supernatural evidence that God was 'On Our Side'. Far from a catastrophe, the retreat from Mons, at least in terms of the moral high ground, was a triumph.

The reality was that on 29 September 1914 the *London Evening News* published a short story called *The Bowmen* by Arthur Machen, a journeyman Welsh writer of both fact and fiction. It was taken to be a first-hand account of events surrounding the retreat from Mons, in which phantom bowmen summoned by a soldier calling on St George for help put the German hosts to flight. The problem was, the piece was not labelled as fiction, while the same issue of the paper had another account clearly headed

'Our Short Story'. As a result, some disorientated readers, suddenly accustomed to reading true reports of events so grotesque and outlandish that they would have been beyond their wildest nightmares only a few weeks earlier, fell upon this as a rare shaft of uplifting news, evidence of a benign force for greater good at work amid the devastation.

For the first time in his life, Machen was in demand. Who were his sources? Could the story be reprinted in parish magazines and as a pamphlet? As a man who owed his living to being a trustworthy correspondent, he had no wish to be branded a hoaxer and made it plain that this was simply fiction taken out of context. Christmas came and went, and none of the illustrated war weeklies made anything of the Angels of Mons. They set their artists to work on all manner of stirring imaginary scenes, from cavalry charges to naval battles and, in the festive numbers, jolly scenes of naval officers and men splicing the mainbrace. But hosts of angels or phantom bowmen hovering in vast protective ranks over sleeping Tommies? It would have been the perfect Christmas angle, and there was not a trace of it to be seen.

In fact it was only in April and May, six months or more after the retreat, that the story suddenly caught fire. Towards the end of April the *British Spiritualist* magazine told of a supernatural force that miraculously intervened at Mons to help the British in their hour of need, and the times were so febrile that the claim unlocked the floodgates. From the gutter press to the pulpits, everybody was talking about the Angels of Mons – including, apparently, friends of friends of soldiers who had suddenly recalled that yes, they had seen them, shimmering bright and watching over them in their retreat. Bowmen? Maybe. Winged beings? Maybe. Joan of Arc? Could have been. One ingenious conspiracy theory was that military intelligence used the story as morale-boosting propaganda at a time when the *Lusitania* had been sunk with appalling loss of life, and the long-feared threat of Zeppelin attacks appeared to be coming true. Obviously, sources for the Angel stories could not be disclosed for security reasons.

A small number of serving soldiers later spoke of visions of phantom cavalrymen, rather than angels or bowmen, during the retreat from Mons, far too late to attack the Germans. Today there is a theory that as they had been on the march for days with neither food nor sleep, these men had simply been hallucinating. A more likely explanation is that as time passed by, a small minority of troops would confuse the story with an understandably blurred recollection of events and think yes, the Angels of Mons; I was there, I must have seen them. The fact is, however, that not a single sighting appears in the regimental history of any of the units involved in the retreat – and nowhere at any time were local newspapers publishing first-hand accounts from young men who would surely have been all too eager to share their close encounter with a protective heavenly host with the anxious folks back home. On the other hand, come the first couple of days of January 1915, editors could have filled their pages twice over with vivid and still disbelieving stories of cigars and Schnapps with Fritz in no-man's-land.

As we have discovered, certain accommodations with the enemy were far from unknown. Along some stretches of the line it was taken as read that it would be quiet at breakfast and maybe other meal times, and besides, come early December, there was a widespread acceptance on each mud-clogged side that there would not be any major action before spring. Over and above this, this was the first Christmas of the war, and who knew how young volunteers at the front were supposed to react in such circumstances? Sufficient men on either side were steeped in the Sunday school tradition to know that this was the time of peace and goodwill, when shooting and killing were anathema. 'Stille Nacht' and 'Silent Night' only served to intensify this feeling, and besides, if there was acceptance that there were times of less intensive hostility towards the enemy, which in day-to-day practical terms there very obviously was, then it would be perverse for Christmas not to be one of those times.

A truce was anything but official policy for either side. General Sir Horace Smith-Dorrien, commander of the British II Corps, issued express orders banning 'unofficial armistices and the exchange of tobacco and other comforts, however tempting and occasionally amusing they might be'. This was no way, it was widely agreed, to nurture the belligerent spirit. The extent to which peace and goodwill were not part of the strategic agenda was shown by the fact that both the British and Germans chose Christmas as the time to launch their first air raids on one another's territory, for what they were worth, the Germans at Dover and the Thames Estuary and the British at Cuxhaven. Fortunately or unfortunately, nobody told Tommy and Fritz in the trenches about that ...

Even within the army, even within the confines of the Western Front, the number of men who fraternised made up quite a tiny section of the whole. Only a minority of the force was at the front, anyway, and most of the interaction took place in and between the trenches around Ypres, over tens of kilometres rather than hundreds. Nevertheless, by the time you were going over the top to meet and greet the foe in a mixture of excitement and apprehension, with men from both sides doing the same as far as the eye could see, it must have seemed truly as if the world had turned upside down. Even the Christmas Day weather had changed from dreary rain to bright sunshine and a sharp white frost. It was the kind of day, a young Warwickshire Regiment officer told his folks, when he could almost have expected to see a little telegraph boy running up with the message:

'War off, return home – George R.I.' Instead, 'it was a nice, fine day, that was all'.

It was largely a case of meeting and chatting, hoping the batch of Jerries you found yourself with included somebody who spoke English. Often enough it did, and in the weeks that followed tales of coincidental meetings, real or imaginary, began to filter into the press: the barber from the Essex Road who cut your uncle's hair, the waiter who served you at the regimental dinner at the Savoy in 1912, the chef at the Trocadero at Piccadilly Circus, the young officer who asked you to post a letter to his girlfriend in Manchester, which when next home on leave you dutifully did.

Football was a passion, then and now, and there is no doubt that there were ad hoc kickabouts with cans of bully beef, sandbags and whatever might come to hand. The fact that the pitch was no-man's-land, with all the limitations to open play that that implies, suggests that most of these would be fairly desultory affairs. The best-documented one, from both sides, was between Medical Corps men, maybe among others, and the 133rd Saxon Regiment. On New Year's Day 1915, an Royal Army Medical Corps major told *The Times* of a cordial meeting with the enemy, after which his men 'actually had a football match with the Saxons, who beat them three-two!!!' The story is amplified in the official war history of the 133rd Saxons, which tells of 'Tommy und Fritz'

Boots with a parade-ground sheen on no-man's-land,
in *The War Budget* artist's version of a meeting of officers in
the Christmas Day truce. Photographs of the men together
paint a rather more bedraggled image. (*The War Budget*,
16 January 1915)

at first joining in a mad chase around cabbage fields chasing hares, and then playing with a ball provided by an obliging Scot: 'This developed into a regulation football match with caps casually laid out as goals ... Then we organised each side into teams, lining up in motley rows, the football in the centre ... The game ended three-two for Fritz.'

It was an eye-opener for other 133rd Saxons when they played a Scots team after duly exchanging Schnapps for rum. 'Our privates soon discovered that the Scots wore no underpants under their kilts, so that their behinds became clearly visible any time their skirts moved in the wind,' Oberleutnant Johannes Niemann recalled in a Hamburg newspaper in 1969. 'We had a lot of fun with that, and in the beginning we just couldn't believe it ...' Farther north, the Lancashire Fusiliers' A Company played Jerry with a ration tin as a ball, with the result again being a 3–2 reverse. At least we can presume that these games were not settled by a penalty shoot-out. There are accounts of several other football matches, and they struck a chord with the public: if only nations' differences could be settled so cleanly, swiftly and painlessly.

For several years a rhyme had been doing the rounds on picture postcards:

> Talk not of war's alarms,
> Football hath greater charms,
> Better than feats of arms

Are feats of feet.
Let then your guns be mute;
Call only those who shoot
Goals with unerring boot
Heroes complete.

A closer approximation of the spirit of the truce, as seen in
a now iconic image published in *The Illustrated War News*
on 20 January 1915, with a goatskin-clad Tommy between
two Saxons. 'In a letter accompanying our photographs,' the
magazine reported, 'a private from the London Rifle Brigade
writes from the Ypres-Armentieres neighbourhood: "I and
some of our pals strolled up from the reserve trenches after
dinner and found a crowd of some hundred Tommies from
each nationality holding a regular mothers' meeting".'
(*The Illustrated War News*, 20 January 1915)

Although the top brass explicitly forbade such behaviour, the German authorities in particular sent out a mixed message by providing their men at the front with thousands of Christmas trees and strings of lights with which to decorate their trenches. On both sides, too, the men were being inundated by gifts and showered with love, even though some of them grumbled that it was not the love they lacked, it was the girl to give it to. Not all the Christmas trees survived unscathed. There were sections where the truce meant nothing, and even in parts where it did, accidents could happen – men picked off by mean-spirited snipers or stray shells landing from positions some way beyond the front line. By and large, however, those who entered into the truce did so wholeheartedly, and emerging feelings towards individuals among the foe – 'They were just like us, hoping it would soon be over, bearing no personal animosity towards us' – were exactly of the kind the authorities feared.

It is the truce, the fraternisation, that is best remembered today – but what is even more remarkable, surely, in two more or less well drilled armies with draconian disciplinary procedures, was the mass disobedience, the mass trespass towards and often enough, particularly among the British, beyond enemy lines. 'We heard the Germans singing "Silent Night, Holy Night" and they put up a notice saying "Merry Christmas" so we put up one too,' Londoner Private Frank Sumpter recalled, continuing:

An *Illustrated War News* picture of Tommies bringing in mistletoe 'swinging from the deadly barrels' of their rifles – 'so rich in suggestion of the happiness of Christmases when the scourge of war was not upon the nations'. (*The Illustrated War News*, 30 December 1914)

When they were singing our boys said 'Let's join in,' so
we joined in and when we started singing they stopped.
And when we stopped, they started again. Then one
German took a chance and jumped up on top of the
trench and shouted, 'Happy Christmas, Tommy!' So of
course our boys said, 'If he can do it, so can we,' and
we all jumped up. A sergeant-major shouted, 'Get down!'
But we said, 'Shut up, Sergeant, it's Christmas time!'
And we all went forward to the barbed wire ... The officers gave the order 'No fraternisation', and then turned
their backs on us. They didn't try to stop it because they
knew they couldn't ...

Private Sumpter is not remembered as a distinguished military commentator, but his assessment
of the situation could not have been more spot-on.
The top brass behind the lines in France knew the
British public would not countenance their husbands,
sons and lovers being punished for doing what they
had been brought up to do by honouring a holy feast
day. Surely, if anyone had earned a day off, it was our
brave boys at the front?

A by-product of the truce was to allow for useful
work to be done, sometimes involving mixed parties
as far as the gathering and burying of the dead was
concerned. At the same time, there were plenty of
young officers who wanted to be out there in the
middle for the same sensation-seeking reasons as their
men did. In fact one of them reported that he was

so disappointed to return to the front on Boxing Day and hear of the fun he had missed that he promptly arranged with his opposite number to extend the truce another twenty-four hours. In some sectors the truce began on 23 December and lasted more or less into the New Year when, as elsewhere, it ended with cheery farewells, random shooting in the air, and the scheduled replacement of the front forces by reinforcements to whom the conviviality had meant nothing.

General Smith-Dorrien, who apparently spent Christmas in 'cushy headquarters' well out of harm's way, blustered predictably when he heard

The *Great Deeds Of The Great War* weekly's caption reads: 'King Pudding arrives. A box of Yuletide eatables being broached by a trio of happy Tommies.' (*T.P.'s Journal Of Great Deeds Of The Great War*, 9 January 1915)

After weeks of rubbishing the idea of a Christmas truce,
the illustrated war magazines suddenly found themselves
having to look back on it in a positive or at least neutral light.
*The War Pictures Weekly* chose to show troops from both sides
burying the dead, rather than exchanging souvenirs: 'Truly
an amazing scene!' (*The War Pictures Weekly*, 21 January 1915)

what had gone on. On Boxing Day evening his
aides had taken him to two sections of the front
that had been of the 'Bah, humbug' school of
thought towards Christmas, but the wool was not
to be pulled over his eyes for long. 'I was shown a
report from one section of how, on Christmas Day,
a friendly gathering had taken place of Germans
and British on the neutral ground between the
two lines, recounting that many officers had taken
part in it,' he wrote in a confidential briefing to his
senior officers.

This is not only illustrative of the apathetic state we
are gradually sinking into, apart also from illustrating
that any orders I issue on the subject are useless, for
I have issued the strictest orders that on no account
is intercourse to be allowed between the opposing
troops. To finish this war quickly, we must keep up the
fighting spirit and do all we can to discourage friendly
intercourse. I am calling for particulars as to names
of officers and units who took part in this Christmas
gathering, with a view to disciplinary action.

Of which, of course, there was none. Where to begin,
where to end? There was evidence against scores,
hundreds, maybe thousands of men, but for once
a system that shot alleged cowards at dawn and
strapped or 'crucified' quite minor offenders to gun
carriage wheels for hours on end was powerless to act
against some rookie private who gave comfort and
succour to the enemy by presenting him with a tin
of His Imperial Majesty's finest bully beef. 'Shut up,
Sergeant, it's Christmas time!' General Smith-Dorrien
wrote the rules, but this was the extraordinary day
when Private Sumpter interpreted them as he saw fit.

Twelve months on, in 1915, by which time relent-
less aggression had expunged any thought of a
widespread armistice, there was the odd case brought
to court marshal, including that of Captain Sir Iain
Colquhoun of the Scots Guards, who had negotiated
a ceasefire to allow men on both sides to bury their

dead, after which they mingled for a few minutes. Colquhoun was 'reprimanded', a sentence instantly remitted by Earl Haig, and he went on to rise to the rank of brigadier general.

The Christmas truce and the football matches in particular have been very much to the fore in several events to mark the centenary of the beginning of the First World War. The English Premier League has financed a floodlit football pitch at Ypres, and this being the Premier League, we are told that it is not just a football pitch but a state-of-the-art third-generation artificial pitch to host a now annual tournament between teams aged under 12 representing leading clubs from England, Belgium, France and Germany; bearing in mind the make-up of the forces in the vicinity a century ago, by rights Scotland, Ireland and India should be in there, too. It need hardly be said that Germans, in the form of Borussia Mönchengladbach, are the current holders of the trophy.

In between times the pitch provides an excellent sports facility for the young people of Ypres, and it is this use that many will see as a more fitting reminder of the spirit of those rag-tag matches of 100 years ago. These games said nothing about the working classes uniting and rising up against the Establishment; but in their artless way they highlighted the absurdity of the situation in which these young men found themselves – and gave them, for the first and last time during the war, the opportunity to express their humanity and fellow-feeling towards the enemy in any great number.

Those times would come (and go, and return) again, but so far as the Great War was concerned, those on both sides quickly grew to recognise that what happened at Christmas 1914 was a fleeting and unique phenomenon, meaningless in the grander scale of things but nevertheless, something quite astonishing in which to have taken part:

> Our revels now are ended. These our actors,
> As I foretold you, were all spirits and
> Are melted into air, into thin air ...

Not many of the lads in the trenches would have claimed to be Shakespearean scholars, but as the years passed by a large number of them grew to look back on their brief encounter on no-man's-land as something as insubstantial as a dream – beyond belief, elusive yet somehow never to be forgotten.

# TRUCE?
# WHAT TRUCE?

Britain's various weekly illustrated magazines so demonised the Germans that it was with embarrassment and in a low key that they reported on the Christmas truce in the trenches, if at all. None was more robust in his personal invective against the enemy than T.P. O'Connor, whose magazine *T.P.'s Journal Of Great Deeds Of The Great War* used every trick in the book to engender hatred towards the Hun.

An odd chap, Thomas Power O'Connor, or Tay Pay as he was often known, mimicking his central Irish accent. An Irish nationalist and busy and successful journalist, he managed to serve as an MP in the British Parliament for nearly fifty years, at first representing various Irish constituencies but later, from 1885 to his death in 1929, the confusingly named seat of Liverpool Scotland, as in the notoriously tough, hard-up, and at that time largely Irish Scotland Road. Hardly surprisingly, this was the only constituency outside Ireland ever to elect an Irish Nationalist MP, and he continued to be returned unopposed under this label in the 1918, 1922, 1923, 1924 and 1929 general elections, by the last of which Irish independence had been a fact of life for half a dozen years, and the Irish Nationalist party had all but ceased to exist after the Sinn Féin landslide of 1918. This remarkable record goes to show what a charismatic character O'Connor was; either that, or maybe it simply tells us that Liverpool Scotland was a deeply weird constituency.

He founded and was the first editor of several newspapers and periodicals, and *Great Deeds Of The Great War* was a spin-off of *T.P.'s Weekly*, which he started in 1902. His seemed an odd background for someone at the helm of a Union Jack-waving, tub-thumping, Bosch-baiting rag, although doubtless his anti-British views had mellowed since his early days as Charles Stewart Parnell's cheerleader in the Home Rule League. Later landmarks along his route to Establishment acceptability included his appointment as the first president of the Board of Film Censors in 1917, a Privy Council post in the first Labour Government in 1924 and finally, the honorary title of Father of the House as the Commons' longest-serving MP.

Back to 9 January 1915, when a long article in his *Great Deeds Weekly* purported to tell the story of Christmas 1914 in the trenches without a single reference to the feared F-word, fraternisation. In O'Connor's account, drawing heavily upon reports from the front by various correspondents, it was universally a case

'There was no Christmas truce at the front,' *The Illustrated War News* reported on 30 December in an issue that clearly went to press days before the 25th. The magazine then claims that this picture shows Tommies cooking their Christmas geese, and since these are such pathetic, scraggy specimens it is cheering to think that this must be equally untrue.
(*The Illustrated War News*, 30 December 1914)

of Tommy doing the best he could to spend Christmas in a seemly manner while the Hun was intent only on desecrating the day. The extracts below tell present-day readers all they need to know about T.P.'s *modus operandi*, but note especially his black arts at work when he manages to turn an innocuous festive greeting from the German High Command into 'merriment by order'. What might well be said about these notices posted in the German trenches is that they helped embolden the men on that side to call the truce, as it is beyond question that most of the first moves came from the Germans. By the time T.P. O'Connor published this piece, stories of the get-togethers in no-man's-land had flooded back to Britain, sent by the men to their families and then passed on to the newspapers. Everybody in the country knew that, for a few hours at least, something extraordinary had happened along some sections of the front. T.P. O'Connor had doubtless not anticipated this turn of events some days earlier, when his magazine had gone to bed. No matter, this was his spin on it all:

Assuredly, never did our men spend a grimmer Christmas than that just over; and yet probably never were the most of them in a happier state of mind, with the sense of duty done to their imperilled and outraged country and people, and with abounding testimony to the warmth of the affection which their kinsmen, near by blood or near by nationality, felt for them. It was a strange medley, this historic Christmas, of all kinds of scenes: joyous and terrible, touching and revolting ...

I start on the Belgian frontier and Northern France, where the Germans ushered in the Birthday of Christ with a particularly violent attack on our forces. There was a hard frost and heavy winter mist, and, as our correspondent puts it, the weather did its best to produce the Christmas atmosphere; but as he goes on to say, the combatants would not take the hint, for this is what happened.

In the early hours of Christmas morning the bombs began to boom on the Yser, showing that there was to be no truce. The Germans made a fierce attack on the French and Belgian positions recently won to the north of Nieuport. The Allies, however, were ready for them, and the German marines were driven back by machine guns and rifle fire, losing many men ... On the British front, things were quieter. Thursday had seen one of the most violent cannonades of the war, but yesterday there was only occasional shelling, and on the whole our men were able to eat their Christmas dinner in peace ...

First, let me note that strangely different temper between our feelings, as represented by our soldiers, and those of malignant and childish hatred, of which we read so much in the German papers. I have always been struck, writes an English correspondent, and never more so than during this Christmastide, by the large-hearted, tolerant attitude our men have unconsciously adopted towards the individual German soldier. 'We only want to meet him and beat him on a purely sporting basis,' said a non-commissioned officer to me this morning, and in so saying, epitomised the creed of his comrades in the field. Malice finds no place at all in the British military equipment, and that is why a season consecrated to goodwill and fellowship finds the hand and heart of the British soldier in sympathy with the Christmas spirit.

And this is how our soldiers showed their spirit in the celebration of the day – and how the Germans showed theirs: Christmas carols were sung in the British trenches. 'Tipperary' was for once in a way ignored. In one instance at least British and German soldiers sang a hymn together – in tune and sentiment, if not in actual words. But no sooner had the carol ended than the cynical Teutonic touch was introduced by a shower of bullets from the enemy trenches.

Merriment to order: let us turn the kaleidoscope and see how the Germans have been celebrating Christ's birthday after their peculiar fashion. They are not forgotten, of course, by their people at home: hundreds of thousands of parcels, says an English correspondent, arrived from Germany, containing knitted articles, sweets, cakes and tobacco. And there was another reason why the Germans should celebrate Christmas joyously; for as the same correspondent writes, the enemy made merry to a military order, for notices were issued several days ago that the troops must do their best to enjoy Yuletide. In that police- and soldier-ridden nation, even joy has to be made to order. And this is the picture we get of what form this officially engineered festival took. It is not altogether edifying, though quite characteristic: there is merrymaking by day and by night, plenty of eating and drinking and the singing of songs, and there has been a general relaxation of discipline to an extraordinary extent in the towns and villages well behind the front.

The Germans feast while the Belgians starve ... It is almost incredible, but it is true, that these carousings have to be paid for by the Belgians, for this is how it has been done. Enormous quantities of wine of all kinds, as well as beer and liqueurs, have been concentrated in the various barracks where the reserve troops have been quartered. The military authorities are giving a certain allowance of drink free, which the men supplement by purchases at absurdly low prices, fixed by the commandant. The usual 'scraps of paper' are given to the Belgian civilians in exchange for their commodities, and many fine private cellars at Liege, Ghent, Bruges, Brussels and Antwerp, which had hitherto escaped the attentions of thirsty officers, have been heavily taxed to supply the Christmas cheer of the invaders ... under penalty of wholesale confiscation and punishment.

And now look at the sadder side of the picture. It makes one's blood boil – but also it strengthens one's resolve: for thousands of destitute Belgians, Christmas Day must have been one of the saddest of their lives by reason of the bitter contrast between their own hopeless plight and the boisterous merriment of the officers and men whose presence means the slow starvation of the populace left in their clutches. Worst of all, perhaps, is the condition of the wretched inhabitants of what were once the chief industrial towns of Belgium. Despite the excellent work of the American relief committee, many persons in Charleroi and Mons had no more than a single piece of bread as food in the twenty-four hours, and the state of Namur is not much better. Thus Christmas means a day of fasting, as well as mental anguish, for the families who are waiting for their deliverance at the hands of the Allies.

As another correspondent admirably sums up the contrast: While the German soldiers were feasting, drinking and roaring wine-songs, the unfortunate Belgians were glad to have a Christmas dinner of half a loaf ...

# CHRISTMAS DINNER
# WITH AN
# AERIAL SHOW

Compared with what was to come in the Second World War, the first air raid on London, on Christmas Day 1914, did not cause much distress to most of the capital's inhabitants. It was Oberleutnant-zur-See Stephan von Prondzynski's second foray over our shores in twenty-four hours, following on from his Christmas Eve visit to Dover, and while he again failed to inflict any serious damage with his single bomb, the mere fact that a seaplane could again pierce Britain's flimsy defences and threaten a strategically important site presented the authorities with fresh concerns.

Prondzynski's target as he flew his Friedrichshafen FF29 up the Thames and Medway estuary on a clear, sunny early afternoon had been London Docks, but it was his exit, rather than the minimal damage he inflicted, that gave the docklands' neighbours a Christmas dinner to remember. 'Few, if any, residents in Dartford imagined they would be entirely forgotten by the Kaiser's emissaries when they arranged their visiting list for this country, and there was therefore no room for surprise when about one o'clock on Christmas afternoon the sounds of heavy firing brought many people to their doors and windows to see what had caused it,' the *Dartford Chronicle* reported on 1 January 1915:

> Watchers on East Hill saw one machine approach the river at great altitude, circle over the town, and then make off in the direction of Gravesend to the accompaniment of reports from all sorts and sizes of guns, and the occasional scream of a shell.
>
> As the enemy passed over Stone, a Vickers biplane soared over the houses from the marshes and gave chase. This was manned by Flight Lieutenant Chidson and Corporal Martin of the Royal Flying Corps, who are stationed at Dartford. It appeared to be gaining on the flying foe as it passed out of sight, and judging from the noise, was keeping up a hot fire. The German was hit at least twice and seen to swerve, and it is thought that two other shots took effect, though it was not possible to bring him down owing to the jamming of the gun with which the British machine was armed.

The FF29 was also fired on from the battery at Sheerness, and when one of its shells fell into a field a couple of miles away at Iwade – inflicting, by good fortune, no damage – the military authorities were given further food for thought.

The sight of a German bomber escaping the attention of British aircraft over the Thames on Christmas afternoon prompted the *Penny War Weekly*'s artist to indulge in his own flight of fancy and show readers what he thought *should* have happened ... (*Penny War Weekly*, 9 January 1915)

The roast beef and plum pudding were also abandoned at the seaside, when 'at 1.35 p.m. yesterday a tremendous firing of guns was heard at Southend,' according to the Press Association's man there. 'People left their Christmas dinner and made for the cliffs, where by means of glasses they saw two large aeroplanes between Southend and Sheerness, proceeding at full speed and at a great height in the direction of the North Sea ... the guns apparently having no effect upon the aircraft.' Since one of them was the Vickers, maybe it was just as well. At Sheerness three more aircraft tried to head off the 'hostile Taube' – a name that had obviously become a generic term for any enemy monoplane – but it flew over Sheppey and was last seen by the Press Association's Sheerness correspondent heading 'in the direction of Shoeburyness, going at a very high speed and apparently making for the East Coast with the object of re-crossing the North Sea. Three machines went up to try to outflank the German aeroplane, but it was flying too fast to allow of the success of the manoeuvre, and it was apparently beyond the range of the anti-aeroplane guns, several of which were fired.'

What the burghers of Dartford, Gravesend, Sittingbourne, Southend, Sheerness and their neigh-bouring communities were watching was the combat debut of the Royal Flying Corps' 'Fighting Biplane' the FB5, better known as the Vickers Gunbus. This was a fearsome name for what to us today would not seem a very fearsome-looking aircraft, with canvas-covered wings and tailplane and a fuselage consisting of nothing more than steel tubes aft of the cockpit. The FB5 had taken its maiden flight only six months previously and the first one was delivered to the Royal Flying Corps little more than a month before Christmas, so the crew had had little time to master its ways. What the onlookers below most certainly did not see that day was a dogfight in the cut-and-thrust tradition of what became a common sight towards the end of this conflict and over into the Second World War. For a start, the Germans were simply intent on bolting for home, rather than engaging the defenders; and secondly, both aircraft were steered laterally by the cumbersome wing warping system, which would very soon become obsolete. Pilots veered away from a straight line at their peril.

The FB5 that engaged Stephan Prondzynski's aircraft was stationed at the RFC's airfield at Joyce Green, on the Dartford Marshes in Kent. It was armed with a Lewis gun firing drum-fed .303-inch bullets, but as the *Dartford Chronicle* reported, this jammed and the gunner resorted to a machine gun rattling out incendiary bullets. The FF29 was clearly hit more than once, and Prondzynski and his observer von Frankenburg must have felt they had well earned their Iron Crosses by the time they reached Zeebrugge again. As for the British pilot, eighteen days later, Second Lieutenant M.R. Chidson – it seems the local newspaper had promoted him a notch or two in its report on the incident – was flying the first Gunbus to operate in France when he was forced to land behind the Kaiser's lines and see the aircraft fall into enemy hands; not a pleasant experience, but there was the comfort that the British could not teach German designers much about aeronautical technology at that time.

# THE CHRISTMAS DAY
## RAID ON
## CUXHAVEN

When the British public came to hear about the Christmas Day naval raid on Cuxhaven, at the mouth of the Elbe – and on major holidays, the Exchange and Telegraph news service was never at its slickest – the immediate reaction was satisfaction that the Germans' bombardment of the north-east English coast nine days earlier had been conclusively and reasonably quickly avenged.

That, however, was only part of the story. What was kept secret from the people until the New Year was the fact that this was the first raid in history in which aircraft launched from ships had taken part in hostile action. 'The Cuxhaven raid marks the first employment of the seaplanes of the Naval Air Service in an attack on the enemy's harbours from the sea, and, apart altogether from the results achieved, it is an occasion of historical moment,' *Flight* magazine, 'The Official Organ of the Royal Aero Club of the United Kingdom' reported some time later. 'Not only so, but for the first time in history a naval attack has been delivered simultaneously above, on and from below the surface of the water.'

The idea was so outlandish that none of the national press's naval correspondents dreamed of accepting this as anything other than a conventional naval bombardment – tit-for-tat, indeed, for the assault on Hartlepool, Scarborough and Whitby. 'This is Britain's answer, in characteristic style, to the bombardment of the Yorkshire Coast,' the *Daily News* purred, while across the Atlantic the *New York Tribune* saw the attack as 'most brilliant and most daring', one that 'put the Hartlepool raid in the shade. It was also free of the stigma of a brutal assault on non-combatants.'

It took days for the true story to come out. Even as late as 29 December the Press Association was reporting the engagement in some detail without a hint of any airborne involvement. Its accounts were truthful, however, in admitting that not a great deal of damage had been done – and there was genuinely good news in that the defences of the German U-boats and Zeppelins, painted in the early days of the war as the enemy's great secret weapons, had been breached and retreated from with no British casualties. 'The submarines constantly attempted to reach the British cruisers, but they were baffled by the masterly seamanship of the destroyers, which manoeuvred at high speed round the larger vessels and successfully repelled every attempt to torpedo them,' the Press Association reported, while adding: 'The Zeppelins had no terrors for the British gunners, who fought as steadily and heartily as if they were fighting sea ships.' The *Daily Chronicle* naval expert's view was: 'Already the much-discussed German submarine is deprived of half its terrors.' That was the way many on this side of the water saw it, a case of terrors faced up to and overcome, and the news could hardly have been more heartening.

When Whitehall argued that Hartlepool played no part in its thinking about Cuxhaven, the press and public found it hard to swallow; surely, the thought must have flitted across the mind of even the most robotic naval planner as the task force steamed across the North Sea from Harwich. The official line, however, was this was an 'air reconnaissance of the Heligoland Bight, including Cuxhaven, Heligoland and Wilhelmshaven ... by naval seaplanes', during which 'the opportunity was taken of attacking with bombs points of military importance'.

Today we can see there is no reason to discount this scenario, except to assume that 'the opportunity of attacking with bombs' was considerably higher up the agenda than was being admitted. On 22 September, the first British air raid against Germany, by Royal Naval Air Service aircraft based in Dunkirk, had targeted Zeppelin bases near Cologne and Düsseldorf, and it was no coincidence that the Nordholz Airbase near Cuxhaven also housed Zeppelin hangars. The negating

The raid on Cuxhaven as it happened only in the imagination of *The War Pictures Weekly*'s artist. (*The War Pictures Weekly*, 7 January 1915)

of the threat of enemy airships was Britain's first bombing priority of the war; from the time civilian German 'blimps' had first passed silently and eerily over southern England in 1910 they had been viewed with apprehension and fear, and eliminating their menace was a major strategic objective. The fact that the number available for military use to the Germans at the beginning of the war amounted to no more than seven was of no comfort to a public bombarded with scare stories.

As Cuxhaven was out of range of English-based aircraft, the navy broke new ground in planning the seaplane attack. Several planned dates for action came and went in October and November, aborted by bad weather, and it was on 2 December that orders were issued to launch the raid at dawn on Christmas Day. A few days into the war, on 13 August, the Admiralty had bought three fast cross-Channel ferries, the *Empress*, *Riviera* and *Engadine*, and it was on these, converted into seaplane tenders, that nine aircraft crossed the North Sea, supported by more than 100 ships and thousands of men.

The temperature was down to zero when the Royal Naval Air Service seaplanes – flimsy two-man open-cockpit Short biplanes each carrying three 20-pound bombs – were lowered into the sea some 40 miles north west of Cuxhaven. Two failed to start in the cold, and others had real difficulty, while the pilots of the seven that made it off the water were well aware of their added loads' threat to their maximum three-hour flight range; soon fog and low cloud were only making matters worse.

It was ninety minutes before the considerable British fleet was detected by the Germans, and when it was, the enemy elected only to harass it with Zeppelins and U-boats. 'Every British ship engaged in the Cuxhaven raid has returned to the base without loss of life or material,' the Press Association noted on 30 December, still, of course, unaware of the seaplane attack.

One report states that the high-angle fire of the *Arethusa* and *Undaunted* damaged one of the Zeppelins badly ... The British ships approached Heligoland in dark, clear weather, promising a successful raid, but fog descended

when they were near the coast. Nevertheless, it was
decided that the raid should proceed. Undoubtedly some
damage was done, including injury to the fortifications
and earthworks. It is doubtful whether any ships were hit.

The *Arethusa*'s and *Undaunted*'s big guns made good
practice against the Zeppelins, many shrapnel shells
bursting around the cars. It seems certain that some hits
were made, but it was insufficient to impair the navigation
of the aircraft. The German airmen's aim was fairly good,
but apparently the nearest bomb fell twenty yards wide.

In fact the German navy's conspicuous absence was
a source of disappointment to the Royal Navy; one
reason for such a considerable task force was to take
the enemy fleet by surprise, tempt it out of harbour
and overwhelm it through sheer weight of numbers.
'The incident suggests that the German navy has either
taken the former battle off Heligoland to heart, or else it
is so doubly or trebly locked behind its booms and dock
gates that it cannot come out within any reasonable
time,' the *Daily Chronicle* suggested, and the no-show
was a source of speculation for some time. It could be
said that had the engagement gone completely to plan
for Britain, it could even have shortened the war. There
was a report that the air raid had led to the greater
part of the German high seas fleet being moved from
Cuxhaven to points along the Kiel Canal, and certainly in its immediate aftermath it was the enemy's
air arm that took the battle to the homeward-bound

British fleet with seaplanes and airships, along with three U-boats. There was a particularly lively skirmish around HMS *Empress*, which found itself lagging behind the formation, but neither side suffered notable damage. 'One destroyer had a hot time, and there were many narrow escapes,' the Press Association reported.

For the seven British seaplane pilots, the raid was a nightmare. Several, having completely lost their bearings, descended from the fog to check their location, only to be met by anti-aircraft fire. With fuel running low they attacked what targets they could, but the damage they inflicted was minimal. One attacked what he took to be a submerging submarine, another a seaplane base, another two light cruisers, a fourth an anti-aircraft site and properties in Wilhelmshaven. One was even said to have hit the Zeppelin base, more by chance than design, but a good many bombs were ditched in the sea as the seven strove to meet their mother ships.

Only three made it back to be recovered; another three landed off the East Frisian island of Norderney where their crews were rescued by the submarine E11 and the aircraft scuttled; and Flight Lieutenant Francis Hewlett's seaplane suffered engine problems that forced him to ditch it into the sea, leaving his colleagues fearing the worst for him and his crewman. Posted as missing, they were in fact picked up by a Dutch trawler and re-emerged safe and well early in the New Year. Against all odds, every man had returned unscathed.

Surviving seaplanes being hoisted aboard their mother ships off Heligoland after the Cuxhaven raid. (*The Illustrated War News*, 30 December 1914)

The Christmas Day seaplane bombing raid on the Zeppelin depot at Cuxhaven was not the greatest military triumph, but the press made a great deal of the rescue of one of the naval airmen, Commander Hewlett, who was picked up by a Dutch trawler after his aircraft had ditched into the North Sea. Here is the event visualised by artists for *The War Budget* (16 January 1915) and *The War Pictures Weekly* (14 January 1915).

War? What war? The caption to this cosy image from
*The Illustrated War News* of 30 December 1914 reads:
'By time-honoured naval usage, on Christmas Day, after
Divine Service, on board every ship, the officers, headed by
the Captain, visit the men at dinner in their messes, which
are always gay with seasonable decorations ...' (*The Illustrated
War News*, 30 December 1914)

Some might say that this hazardous operation was
scarcely an unqualified success, with no Zeppelins
or major installations destroyed and the planned-for
drubbing of the German Navy a forlorn hope. But
Cuxhaven showed the Royal Navy and Royal Naval Air
Service that they had the organisation and resources
to combine to strike at the heart of the enemy's most
heavily guarded sites, and pose an on-going threat to
the Zeppelin campaign. Add a dash of Admiralty propaganda and press flag-waving, and here was a Christmas
good news story that would last some way into 1915.

# BRADFORD'S
# GREAT ESCAPISM

It would have taken more than a mere world war to throw the music hall and cinema impresarios off the scent of some bumper Christmas box office takings, and many theatre-goers felt that the dark times in which they were living only served to intensify the colour, verve and spectacle of the halls. Besides, while a million young men had answered Kitchener's call in the five months between August and December, hundreds of thousands more were ready to volunteer after snatching just one more Christmas at home with their loved ones. A special time, then – and how better to celebrate it than a trip to the panto or the picture show?

Bradford in Yorkshire was always a city that enjoyed a show, as it still does, and there was a special buzz about the place at Christmas that year. Two major new venues had opened in 1914, the Alhambra in March and the Regent Theatre (which was always a cinema) in September, while the Theatre Royal was beating the drum about its fiftieth anniversary, its

'Golden Jubilee', as it grandly called it, which fell on Boxing Day. With three other big Christmas shows on in town in opposition to the Royal and Alhambra and the Regent competing with half-a-dozen picture houses showing the latest films, there was plenty of competition for the customers' pennies and shillings.

The Theatre Royal's big show, for two weeks only, was *Peter Pan*, obviously aimed at children and apparently very successful in amusing them. It was only ten years since the play was first produced, while its author, J.M. Barrie, was still at the height of his powers, in his mid-50s and newly knighted by George V. From the

Halfway to its century: the splendid Alhambra in Bradford, now a major venue for touring West End shows and cultural events, seen fifty years ago in 1964. (Bradford Metropolitan District Council)

play's earliest times Peter was played by a young woman, though in a russet red coat and green trousers rather than the neat little green two-piece usually seen today. So popular was the Royal's production, the Bradford *Telegraph & Argus* noted that 'numerous visitors from Wakefield, Leeds and other towns in the neighbourhood' were to be found in the audience.

Until the Alhambra came along, the Prince's and the Empire were the city's most popular variety halls, but now they had stiff competition. 'The top line in a capital programme this week at the Alhambra is the mystery gun, one of those perplexing tricks of which the public never seem to tire,' the *Telegraph & Argus* reported. 'To pass a living being out of a horizontal tube through a steel plate is the undertaking of a naval inventor, who thus wagers to win an admiral's daughter. He wins the wager, and the mystery remains unsolved.' Mini-plays were now becoming quite a feature of variety bills, especially if they involved some mystifying smoke and mirrors.

Sixteen step-dancers who had recently appeared before the King then took centre stage, 'trained to a split fraction', and the reporter was particularly impressed by a Henley Regatta routine in which they danced 'together and in sections and couples through a most enjoyable series of waltzes, unison-stepping lines and athletic movements'. Top of the bill, as she often was in not-quite-stellar-class variety all over the country, was Queenie Essex, with her 'well-managed and telling soprano voice'. Queenie appeared in her own stage setting – 'quite a common feature of hall turns, now' – and the joshing relationship between her and her accompanist put the audience in mind of the This and That act with which the genuine headliner Clarice Mayne was then doing the rounds with her pianist-composer husband James W. Tate (to whom, let it not be forgotten, the world remains grateful for such timeless numbers as 'I Was A Good Little Girl Till I Met You' and 'Put On Your Ta-Ta Little Girlie').

This and That also played a part in the next act on the Alhambra's bill, the perky young Australian comedy impressionist sisters Lorna and Toots Pounds. Then fairly new to Britain but big for a couple of decades afterwards, they had a huge hit at London Palladium in the early 1920s in revue with *Rockets*, and starred in the 1922 Royal Variety Performance. Lorna and Toots would impersonate anybody, and while it is easy to see why the Bradford audience loved their Clarice Mayne spoof, it is harder to imagine how their Harry Tate routine worked. Two Aussie striplings guying the decidedly middle-aged male Tate, with his rotating moustache and sketches about motoring, billiards and fishing? Those two must have had some stage presence to carry that off.

There then followed La Triska with her 'admirable doll impersonations' and the singer Tom E. Dean, who 'got several recalls for his well memorised and clearly sung medley of most of the available songs of the day', before the show ended with a little circus in which trained ponies and a big donkey were the top draws. In summary, 'the company made side-splitting fun in front of a crowded house'.

The variety bills at the Prince's, Empire and Palace offered fare at a similar standard. *Aladdin* was the panto at the Prince's, headed by the Yorkshire-born Mona Vivian, who had been on the boards since the age of 4, when 'Wee Mona' won everybody's heart in the panto at Wakefield Hippodrome. She was tops as a dancer, clog dancer, singer and yodeller, talents which doubtless were uppermost in the mind of the million-aire mill owner J. Hilton Crowther, one-time chairman of Leeds United, who married her shortly after the war. At the Prince's she led a female cast that also took in the Misses Minnie Myrle, Aimee Stewart and Cecile De Banke, all of whom naturally 'won the hearts of all who saw them'. 'Genuine fun' was delivered via Messrs Reg Bolton, Will Lindsay, Norman H. Lee, Harry Mills and James Chippendale, while a 'bevy of clever and pretty young children' also pleased. Between them, this cast 'kept the house in a good humour for four hours'. Four hours: a lot of panto, that.

Headliner in the Empire's show was the Scots actress Jean Aylwin, who was 'the Lady Harry Lauder' to some. Her show within a show at that time was *A Careless Lassie*, a yarn about the daughter of a staunchly and strictly religious Scottish family who scandalised her parents by running away to be a music-hall artist, only

to cheer them up somewhat when she married a mil-
lionaire. Maybe the then unmarried Mona Vivian over
at the Prince's caught a matinee show at the Empire
one afternoon and thought 'Hmmm, now there's an
idea.' Also on the bill were the rifle shooting act the
Vivians (presumably no relation), who offered to pass
on their skills to 'any civilian or soldier' at the theatre
each afternoon, even providing their own rifles and
ammunition. As the show ended with 'pictures from
the seat of war', it sounds as if this was not the most
escapist night out in town.

All was fun and games at the Palace, however,
where Hal Jones led a gang of 'nutty cracksmen' in
*The Three Crooks*, and another major draw for 'lovers
of the artistic' was Gaby Revette, with her 'series
of delightful tableaux representative of well-known
works of art and also of original scenes'. This sounds
suspiciously like those female 'living statues' who
helped sound the death knell of variety in the 1940s
and 1950s, though presumably with more clothes on.
Whatever, the *Telegraph & Argus* opined 'the theme is
a capital one, and met with cordial recognition'.

Bradford's second major new venue of 1914,
the ornate and splendid Regent Theatre in Manningham
Lane, strove hard to be a cut above a mere cinema,
with facilities including a café and winter garden, both
of which were buzzing that first Christmas. The main
seasonal offering was *Christmas Day In The Workhouse*,
based on George R. Sims's scathing mid-Victorian

indictment of poverty and hypocrisy, but the *Telegraph & Argus* man was obviously more familiar with the many silly parodies that had come along since then. 'A very entertaining story,' he surmised it would be; this for a film with the synopsis: 'A pauper tells workhouse visitors of his wife's death from starvation.' Not quite festive fare, though perhaps Charlie Chaplin's latest piece, *Caught In A Cabaret*, would have helped send the crowd out laughing.

A century has passed since the Alhambra and the Regent opened with such high hopes, and the Theatre Royal made commercial capital of its fiftieth birthday. The Royal later became a cinema while in 1949 the Regent became the Essoldo, but both are now long gone. The Essoldo ceased trading in 1965 and the building saw various reincarnations as a bingo club and Bollywood cinema before finally closing after a fire in 1975 and later being demolished. The Royal, which was named the Alexandra Theatre when it opened in 1864, turned to films full-time in 1921 and suffered final years very similar to those of the Regent. Bankrupt in 1965, it reopened as the Irving Royal early in 1967, became the Classic Royal later that year and struggled on until late in 1974. It then stood derelict and fell to the demolition balls after being declared unsafe in 1990.

And then there is the Alhambra, in rude good health to celebrate its centenary in 2014 and well established as one of Britain's leading venues for tours of the big West End blockbusters as well as companies such as the Royal Shakespeare, Birmingham Royal Ballet, Northern Ballet Theatre and Royal National Theatre. It was refurbished in 1986 to highlight the splendour of its original design, while being able to accommodate all the technical demands of today's major touring shows. Hard though it might be to believe, the tricks they come up with today with scenery, sound and lighting would put even the adorable Queenie Essex's custom-built set of 1914 in the shade.

# THE PLUNGE
## OF THE
## NIGHT HAWK

*Night Hawk* was a minesweeper with a threatening nocturnal name, but it was in broad daylight on Christmas afternoon, 1914 that she met her fate doing the job for which she had been requisitioned. Six months earlier she had been plying her trade in the North Sea as a Grimsby trawler – not light and easy work, by any means, but one in which her crew was confident she was well equipped. After all, she was only 3 years old, she was as state of the art as it was possible to be, and that was doubtless why she found herself called to the colours.

Christmas Day came nine days after the naval bombardment of East Coast towns, including Scarborough, which so shocked the nation. The alien-sounding names of the two battle cruisers that pounded the seaside resort that morning were on everybody's lips, the *Von der Tann* and the *Derrflinger*, but there was a third, smaller vessel that came over from Heligoland with them that night, the light cruiser *Kolberg*. Hers were not the cannons blazing out in the bay that day, but in the longer term she was by far the most deadly of the unwelcome trio.

Her task was to lay 100 mines off Flamborough Head – the densest minefield in the history of naval warfare, according to some. One theory is that the bombardment was merely a distraction from the real purpose of the visit. Another is that the Germans hoped their outrageous action off the Hartlepools, Scarborough and Whitby would lure the British Grand Fleet into those waters, where the mines would have a devastating effect. That did not happen, but many merchant vessels disappeared in the North Sea during the war, never to be found, and it is beyond doubt that some at least of these were victims of the deadly crop sown by the *Kolberg*. As it was, dozens of known ships and hundreds of men perished as a result of her work that 16 December.

Before the end of that day three small merchant ships had been sunk: the first, at just after six in the evening, was the *Elterwater*, a Newcastle collier heading for London, but in quick succession after her came another collier, the *Vaaren*, from Bergen in Norway, and the Liverpool-registered *Princess Olga*, a tramp steamer carrying general cargo. Twenty seamen lost their lives, fourteen on the *Vaaren* and six the *Elterwater*; the *Princess Olga*'s crew lived to tell the tale.

It was three days later when a group of minesweeping trawlers reached the scene, the *Night Hawk* among them. Three more of the converted Grimsby fishing boats were lost in this desperately dangerous work, but she is the one best remembered today, through having the misfortune to be sunk on Christmas Day. In fact that was a lethal day in the minefield, with three dozen men losing their lives in four sinkings: six aboard the *Night Hawk*; ten on the *Gem*, a Glasgow coaster carrying salt cake from Mostyn in North Wales to Tyneside; and twenty-one on the London-registered *Therese Heymann*, a 2,000-ton schooner-rigged steamship heading from Tyneside with coal for Savona, Italy. The fourth vessel, the Bergen-registered collier *Eli*, heading from Blyth for Rouen, sank with no loss of life.

No trace of the *Therese Heymann* or her crew was ever found; the ship was not officially classed as missing/untraced until March 1915, and even a Board of Trade wreck enquiry in August that year came to no firm conclusion. 'From the time that the pilot quitted the *Therese Heymann* off Sunderland, nothing whatever has been heard of that vessel,' the inspector noted. 'In fact, she disappeared from knowledge as completely as if she had never existed.'

And then there was the *Night Hawk*, which lost its chief engineer, second engineer, two trimmers or stokers, a deck hand and a cook, all of them serving in the Royal Naval Reserve. Theirs was a harrowing tale and it did not take long to be told, since the *Scarborough Mercury*'s account of the inquest in the town on the chief engineer, Alfred Chappell, spared no detail.

The newspaper reported:

The Coroner said that the *Night Hawk* came into contact with a submerged mine. Several of the men were blown completely out into the sea by the explosion, and some sank with the ship. It was simply a sequel to the bombardment, an event which had never occurred so far as he was aware at any time before ... He had never heard of any bombardment of a practically helpless town the same as Scarborough. If his information was right, these mines which had been floating about in the Bay were laid down by the enemy ships at the bombardment. That made the bombardment all the more terrible and ruthless, and all the more disgraceful. (Hear, hear.) The course of this war would appear to be carried on in a different way to that most civilised countries had been accustomed to and expected ...

The first witness was Harry Evans of Grimsby, the skipper; still with his forehead heavily bandaged he said the minesweeping fleet was working from north to south and back between Flamborough Head and Whitby:

We left Whitby at 7 a.m. on Christmas Day, working southward. We were three-and-a-half to four miles from Scarborough when we struck this mine, which exploded at once. If was like a deafening concussion as if we had struck a rubber ball. I think the whole of the bottom must have been knocked out. Everything was blown to pieces. From the stern to amidships was almost completely blown up.

He was asked why the explosion was at the stern of the vessel, and replied: 'We are likely to catch a mine anywhere in the ship. If a surface mine we would be hit on the bow. If a submerged mine, one part of the vessel might pass over and the deeper stern part be caught ...'

The *Mercury* reported that Mr Evans had said that two stokers, the second engineer, the steward and the deck hand had all been below:

We knew nothing about them. In seven or ten seconds after the explosion, she went down. Those below must have fallen through the bottom with the machinery, and it would be instant death. Those of us on deck were either knocked into the water or taken under by suction. With the exception of myself, no one was injured of those on deck, and my injury is only superficial. When we got into the water we would be from fifty to sixty yards apart. There were several other ships sweeping behind us. I think it would be twenty-five minutes to half an hour before assistance arrived. We were struggling in the water that time ... You cannot run other vessels into danger where one has come to grief. The only thing you can do is to send small boats out, and that is how we were picked up. I remember nothing till we returned to the harbour. They tell me I was walking about on the ship whose boat rescued me, but I don't remember anything about it. It was bitterly cold. We each had on a life-belt, a life-jacket and a life-collar.

Alfred Chappell, the chief engineer, who was married with four children, was the only one of the deck crew thrown into the water who did not survive. The inquest heard he was not apparently injured when he was picked up, but seemed to have died from exhaustion. The coroner returned a verdict of death from the effects of shock and exhaustion following the explosion of a mine.

And that would have been the end of the story if the *Daily Telegraph*, to mark the centenary of the outbreak of the First World War, had not asked its readers for anecdotes that had been passed down through their family. Mrs Carol Senior from Harpenden, Hertfordshire, related a story about her husband's grandfather, Lieutenant W.E. Senior of the Royal Naval Reserve, who was commander of the *Night Hawk*, presumably as distinct from the skipper, Harry Evans. 'She hit a mine on Christmas Day and from a crew of thirteen, seven survived, of whom Lieutenant Senior was one. The ship went down in ten seconds,' Mrs Senior wrote to the newspaper, going on to say that the lieutenant was later awarded the Distinguished Service Cross and the Croix de Guerre for his service to minesweeping before eventually becoming dockmaster at Grimsby: 'I felt this episode of the war was very rarely mentioned,' she concluded. 'In Grandpa Senior's honour, the Croix de Guerre sword is used at family weddings to cut the cake.'

# A 'SPANKING'
# CHRISTMAS

As an orderly in the St John Ambulance Brigade, W.M. Floyd served in hospitals in France from September to December 1914. As his diary recorded, a highlight of his service was the 'spanking' Christmas he spent on the wards:

Had spanking Xmas. All paid 2 francs to make extra treat of it. Xmas day arrived, was on night duty. Went to bed straight from duty until 11 a.m. Got up brushed up a bit extra. Dinner 2.30 p.m. Special tent erected decorated up for occasion. General tariff as follows. First course Turkey, brussel sprouts, potatoes, 2nd Xmas pudding. 3rd milk pudding & jellies. Finale fruits etc. muscatels, cigarettes, bananas, apples, etc. etc. After dinner took stroll down town, where all was crowded and gay. In night had small concert. Received present at dinner. Box of chocolates (milk) from the king, packet of cigarettes, pkt tobacco, and Xmas card from Princess Mary in art box.

Feet very firmly on the ground for these nurses at a military hospital in the south of England. (Author's collection)

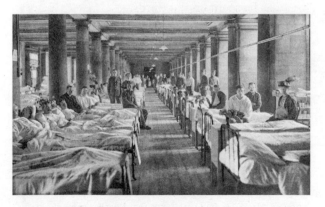

Rank on rank of beds at the military hospital in the cloisters of Trinity College, Cambridge, the Alma Mater of Sir John French, commander of the British Expeditionary Force in France. (*The Illustrated War News*, 11 November 1914)

Recd present case of lead pencils from Miss Karr,
2 francs from sister to buy chocolates. One of the sisters
taking photo of dinner party after climbing on top of
two boxes [descended] from top with more haste than
dignity but luckily didn't hurt herself, shouts of encore
met with no response. Officer supplied gramophone for
amusement. Speech made by colonel and few others.
Ward all decorated out with holly, mistletoe, colour
paper etc. Also Xmas tree loaded with toys like they
do for kids. New carpet put down, coloured shades put
around electric globes give fairylike scenery. Red blankets put on beds instead of black ones looked very pretty.
This Xmas passed with all working hand-in-hand and
complete absence of any bitter feeling that somehow a
man might expect to find in such a large hospital run by
three distinct societies.

# ROAST HORSE AND BOILED POTATOES

Violetta Thurston, born Anna Violet Thurstan
in Hastings in 1879, was a doctor's daughter who
became one of the most high-profile of Britain's wartime nurses, working in Belgium, Poland, France and
elsewhere and keeping the nursing and more general
press up to date with her exploits through almost
weekly letters. Educated in France, Germany and at
St Andrews University in Scotland, she trained as a
nurse at the London Hospital and a children's hospital in Shadwell, East London; by the time the war
began, however, she had moved away from practical
nursing and had established herself as an adminis-
trator, informed commentator and lecturer.

All that went by the board in the autumn of 1914,
when at the age of 35 she reverted to front-line
nursing, having been asked by St John Ambulance
to lead a party of nurses to Brussels to work with
the Belgian Red Cross. The Germans ordered
all foreign nurses to leave the city when it fell,

escorting them across Germany to Copenhagen in neutral Denmark; but there, instead of taking the next ship home, she read of the plight of the Poles, 'the Belgians of Russia', and offered her services to the Russian Red Cross.

They welcomed her, and after reaching Poland by a circuitous route via Lapland and Sweden, she was posted to a hospital in a former girls' school in the densely populated city of Lodz, which fell to the Germans on 6 December 1914. Meticulous in her duties, she still found time to pour out her accounts of her experiences, and astonishingly quickly, in April 1915, the London and New York publishers G.P. Putnam's Sons put out her book *Field Hospital And Flying Column*. Subtitled *Being the Journal of an English Nursing Sister in Belgium & Russia* it was strikingly topical – so much so that it was able to include this account of her experiences just four months earlier, at Christmas 1914.

We had left Zyradow rather quiet, but when we came back we found the cannon going hard, both from the Radzivilow and the Goosof direction. It would have taken much more than cannon to keep us awake, however, and we lay down most gratefully on our stretchers in the empty room at the Red Cross Bureau and slept. A forty-eight hours' spell is rather long for the staff, though probably there would have been great difficulty in changing the Columns more often.

I woke up in the evening to hear the church bells
ringing, and remembered that it was Christmas Eve
and that they were ringing for the Midnight Mass,
so I got up quickly. The large church was packed with
people, every one of the little side chapels was full and
people were even sitting on the altar steps. There must
have been three or four thousand people there, most
of them of course the people of the place, but also
soldiers, Red Cross workers and many refugees, mostly
from Lowice. Poor people, it was a sad Christmas for
them – having lost so much already and not knowing
from day to day if they would lose all, as at that time
it was a question whether or not the Russian authorities would decide for strategic reasons to fall back
once more.

And then twelve o'clock struck and the Mass began.

Soon a young priest got up into the pulpit and gave
them a little sermon. It was in Polish, but though
I could not understand the words, I could tell from
the people's faces what it was about. When he spoke
of the horrors of war, the losses and the deaths and
the suffering that had come to so many of them, one
woman put her apron to her face and sobbed aloud
in the tense silence. And in a moment the whole con-
gregation began sobbing and moaning and swaying
themselves to and fro. The young priest stopped and
left them alone a moment or two, and then began to
speak in a low, persuasive voice. I do not know what
he said, but he gradually soothed them and made

them happy. And then the organ began pealing out triumphantly, and while the guns crashed and thundered outside, the choir within sang of peace and goodwill to all men.

Christmas Day was a very mournful one for us, as we heard of the loss of our new and best automobile, which had just been given as a present to the Column. One of the boys was taking it to Warsaw from Skiernevice with some wounded officers, and it had broken down just outside the village. The mud was awful, and with the very greatest difficulty they managed to get it towed as far as Rawa, but had to finally abandon it to the Germans, though fortunately they got off safely themselves. It was a great blow to the Column, as it was impossible to replace it, these big ambulance cars costing something like eight thousand roubles.

So our Christmas dinner, eaten at our usual dirty little restaurant, could not be called a success. Food was very scarce at that time in Zyradow; there was hardly any meat or sugar, and no milk or eggs or white bread. One of us had brought a cake for Christmas from Warsaw weeks before, and it was partaken of on this melancholy occasion without enthusiasm. Even the punch made out of a teaspoonful of brandy from the bottom of Princess' flask, mixed with about a pint of water and two lumps of sugar, failed to move us to any hilarity. Our menu did not vary in any particular from that usually provided at the restaurant, though we did feel we might have had a clean cloth for once.

Menu - Christmas 1914

Gravy Soup

Roast Horse, Boiled Potatoes

Currant Cake

Tea Punch

After this account of a rather dismal Christmas dinner, Violetta describes a visit to their old dressing-station and even a trip to the front line to provide some Christmas cheer to the men there:

We were very glad to go up to Radzivilow once more. Our former dressing-station had been abandoned as too dangerous for staff and patients, and the dressing- and operating-room was now in a train about five versts down the line from Radzivilow station. Our train was a permanency on the line, and we lived and worked in it, while twice a day an ambulance train came up, our wounded were transferred to it and taken away, and we filled up once more. We found things fairly quiet this time when we went up. The Germans had been making some very fierce attacks, trying to cross the river Rawka, and therefore their losses must have been very heavy, but the Russians were merely holding their ground, and so there were comparatively few wounded on our side. This time we were able to divide up into shifts for the work – a luxury we were very seldom able to indulge in.

We had previously made great friends with a Siberian captain, and we found to our delight that he was living in a little hut close to our train. He asked me one day if I would like to go up to the positions with him and take some Christmas presents round to the men. Of course I was more than delighted, and as he was going up that night and I was not on duty, the general very kindly gave permission for me to go up too. In the end Colonel S. and one of the Russian Sisters accompanied us as well. The captain got a rough cart and horse to take us part of the way, and he and another man rode on horseback beside us. We started off about ten o'clock, a very bright moonlight night – so bright that we had to take off our brassards and anything that could have shown up white against the dark background of the woods.

We drove as far as the pine woods in which the Russian positions were, and left the cart and horses in charge of a Cossack while we were away. The general had intended that we should see the reserve trenches, but we had seen plenty of them before, and our captain meant that we should see all the fun that was going, so he took us right up to the front positions. We went through the wood silently in single file, taking care that if possible not even a twig should crackle under our feet, till we came to the very front trenches at the edge of the wood. We crouched down and watched for some time. Everything was brilliantly illuminated by the moonlight, and we had to be very careful not to show ourselves. A very fierce German attack was going on, and the bullets were pattering like hail on the trees all round us. We could see nothing for some time but the smoke of the rifles.

The Germans were only about a hundred yards away from us at this time, and we could see the river Rawka glittering below in the moonlight. What an absurd little river to have so much fighting about. That night it looked as if we could easily wade across it. The captain made a sign, and we crept with him along the edge of the wood, till we got to a Siberian officer's dug-out. At first we could not see anything, then we saw a hole between two bushes, and after slithering backwards down the hole, we got into a sort of cave that had been roofed in with poles and branches, and was absolutely invisible a few steps away. It was fearfully hot and frowzy—a little stove in the corner threw out a great heat, and the men all began to smoke, which made it worse.

We stayed a while talking, and then crawled along to visit one of the men's dug-outs, a German bullet just missing us as we passed, and burying itself in a tree. There were six men already in the dug-out, so we did not attempt to get in, but gave them tobacco and matches, for which they were very grateful. These men had an 'ikon' or sacred picture hanging up inside their cave; the Russian soldiers on active service carry a regimental ikon, and many carry them in their pockets too. One man had his life saved by his ikon. He showed it to us; the bullet had gone just between the Mother and the Child, and was embedded in the wood.

It was all intensely interesting, and we left the positions with great reluctance, to return through the moonlit pine woods till we reached our cart. We had indeed made a night of it, for it was five o'clock in the morning when we got back to the train once more, and both the doctor and I were on duty again at eight. But it was well worth losing a night's sleep to go up to the positions during a violent German attack. I wonder what the general would have said if he had known!

Violetta Thurston continued to lead an extraordinary life after Poland. She was awarded the Military Medal for bravery after being injured while nursing at the front in France, and on the day after the war ended, on 12 November 1918, she enlisted in the Women's Royal Air Force and found herself administering Arab refugee camps. Other public roles followed in Europe and elsewhere, while at the same time she turned to producing textile designs to international museum standard and adding novels to her list of literary genres. An obituarist, after she had died in 1978 at the age of 97, opined that 'her fragile appearance masked an indomitable spirit'. Reading her account of Christmas 1914, most would feel that the description 'indomitable' sold her considerably short.

# CHRISTMAS DAY
# IN THE WORKHOUSE

First World War Christmases are still within the living memory of a handful of people, yet some newspaper reports from that time read more like chronicles from Victorian Britain. In a way, even the most monstrous action in the theatres of war is more comprehensible to us as twentieth-century behaviour than some of the attitudes of the day on the Home Front.

True, no Western government today would dare to be so wasteful of the lives of its own subjects; at the beginning of 2014, fewer than 450 UK personnel had died in Afghanistan since 2001; 179 were killed in Iraq between 2003 and 2012. But images on our television screens over recent years of street-to-street fighting and exchanged artillery fire in those countries, the former Yugoslavia, the Middle East, Africa and elsewhere tell us that the 1914–18 conflict still has parallels in the world today, however much the technology of warfare might have changed.

Then there was the way we treated our poor, and here we enter another world. By the early twentieth century, workhouses were not as they had been; in providing free medical care and education for children, not to mention regular food, a weatherproof roof and relative safety, they offered most of their inmates a more congenial environment than they might have had to look forward to on the outside. Nevertheless, attitudes towards them had hardly moved on from Dickens's day, and up and down the country Christmas Day in the workhouse was as recognisable as it had been when George Robert Sims wrote his fierce indictment of the Poor Law system in 1879. The reports below appeared in the *Bristol Times and Mirror* on Boxing Day 1914, but there were similar stories in local newspapers all over Britain. The first is from the Eastville Workhouse:

The Bristol Guardians, always considerate of their charges, thought it advisable this year, in view of the especially adverse circumstances existing in this country, not to spend too lavishly on decorations in the institutions, however cheering they might be under normal conditions, but to purchase additional fruit instead; therefore the usually fine decorations of the festive season were not so much in evidence this year, though what was done was carried out with a great deal of thought and care. Evergreens and festoons were utilised in the various wards at Eastville, but there was an absence of the usual mottoes of the humorous or pertinent type.

The children were specially catered for. In the nursery and for young imbeciles, and for the babies in the hospital, there were Christmas trees on which were placed toys for distribution. Gifts were sent from outside friends in a satisfactory way, and the special fare for the 1,100 or so inmates (lower in number than last year) consisted of roast beef, roast pork, two kinds of vegetables or plum pudding, tobacco for the men, oranges or bananas for the women and sweets for the children. One of the ex-chairmen of the Board of Guardians, Mr J. Fanson, who is ill at present, with kindly thought for the aged people provided tea and sugar for the women and tobacco for the men.

The Christmas Day service was conducted by the chaplain, the Revd S. Marle, and an impromptu concert was also given in the day by officers and inmates of the institution. The arrangements were in the charge of the master, Mr T.R. Lambert, and the matron, Mrs A.M. Lambert.

A similar number of people were served at Stapleton Workhouse – 530 men, ten fewer women and ninety children – while at Long Ashton, the *Times and Mirror*'s correspondent sounded rather more upbeat:

It is surprising how a little holly and evergreens, tastefully arranged and used in conjunction with illuminated mottoes and coloured paper decorations, can transform a place and give it a bright and festive appearance ...

The hall was decorated with seasonable greetings and photographs of the King and Queen occupied prominent positions, while in the various rooms the window ledges were lined with evergreens and holly, and the walls adorned with mottoes in gold and white letters on a red ground, within prettily stencilled borders.

In all there were reports from a dozen institutions, several of which had become more recognisable as infirmaries or hospitals rather than workhouses. As the years had passed, workhouses had increasingly become refuges for the elderly, weak or sick rather

Christmas Day in a workhouse men's infirmary ward, with quite generous decorations and the uplifting seasonal mottoes by which the authorities set great store. (Author's collection)

than the able-bodied poor, but it was not until 1929 that legislation was passed to allow local authorities to take over the workhouse infirmaries. In the following year workhouses themselves were formally abolished by the same legislation, though many continued as local authority public assistance institutions until the National Assistance Act of 1948 swept away the last vestiges of the Poor Law.

A new dimension in 1914 was the presence of injured soldiers in the hospitals. At Cossham Memorial Hospital in Keynsham there were twenty-two British and Belgian casualties spread over two wards: 'Patriotic flags and mottoes were used there, some of the latter being "Success To Our Boys On Land And Sea" and "Glory To Those Who Fall On The Field Of Honour".' The feelings of those who had seen all too much of the 'Field Of Honour' can only be imagined. Keynsham Workhouse and Fishponds Asylum also saw their evergreens and festoons, while Kingswood Reformatory enjoyed – the word can almost be taken literally – a busy Christmas Day:

> There are 125 boys at present, the number being much below the full complement as thirty boys have joined the colours since the war started. Several members of the staff who were reservists have been called up again. On Christmas Day a number of Old Boys visited the school, some of whom are back from the front and have fortunately recovered from their wounds. A pleasant

feature of the festivities was that the Old Boys in the fighting line had not been forgotten, as the present scholars had knitted and dispatched a large consignment of woollen scarves and other useful articles ... Altogether, this school has nearly three hundred Old Boys serving with the colours on land and sea, and greetings were received from many of them at the front and in India. The loss of three of these killed in action is much to be deplored.

The lads at the institution had their usual Christmas breakfast of sausages and bacon, and the dinner on Christmas Day was roast beef and plum pudding followed by nuts, sweets and oranges. The lads paraded in the morning for service at Holy Trinity Church, Kingswood, the band playing en route. Football was indulged in in the afternoon, and in the evening a conjuring entertainment was given by a Bristol gentleman.

If this report is to be believed the boys of the Kingswood Reformatory must have enjoyed a fuller Christmas Day, with more food, fun and fellowship, than tens of thousands of other Bristol citizens that day; and the way the Old Boys returned in some numbers suggests that for many who passed through its doors, this, for better or worse, really was the place they had come to regard as home.

# PRISONERS' CHRISTMAS HOLIDAY IN SOUTHEND

Less than five months before Christmas 1914 Britain had been at peace, and the speed with which life had moved on since early August was bewildering on many levels. A small example of the meticulous organisation that was put into the military operation across the board was the provision made for the 3,000 or so German prisoners of war and internees kept in three detention ships moored off Southend. The first of these men had arrived no more than five weeks earlier, in mid-November, and it might be imagined that merely keeping them secure and in relative comfort would have been the extent of the authorities' plans for Christmas.

Far from it, since they 'were provided with substantial fare,' according to a national newspaper quoted in the *Great Deeds Of The Great War* magazine of 9 January 1915. 'For some days boxes and hampers had been arriving – gifts from relatives and friends. There are a thousand military prisoners in the *Ivernia* and two thousand civilian internees in the *Royal Edward* and the *Saxonia*. Among the latter are two wealthy Germans, who between them gave one hundred pounds' worth of cigars. The newspaper went on to record the various luxuries dispatched from the pier:

> One hundred tons of general provisions, including beef and mutton; one hundred barrels of beer; one ton of apples, oranges and nuts; fifty large packages of tobacco and cigars, weighing about two-and-a-half tons; a large quantity of holly, mistletoe and other material for decoration; and several large Christmas trees. The day was spent with music, cards, chess and dominoes. There are pianos, and the prisoners were allowed to sing German songs to their hearts' content.

A great deal of logistical effort must have gone into these arrangements, not least in transporting the gifts from the Fatherland safely across the Channel to a British seaside town whose principal tourist attraction, apart from the longest pleasure pier in the world, was an amusement complex rejoicing in the distinctly Germanic name of the Kursaal. For a brief spell, however, it seemed as if expense was no object in housing the prisoners and internees, with the Cunard Line charging big money for the lease of the *Ivernia* and *Saxonia* and the Canadian Northern Steamship Company being well compensated for the use of the *Royal Edward*, the largest of the three. In fact by the late spring of 1915 the men had been transferred to

A draft of nearly a thousand German prisoners of war arrived at Southend in early December 1914. From the start, the plan was to get them off the detention ships into land-based camps as quickly as possible. (*The Illustrated War News*, 9 December 1914)

land camps near Southend, where they remained for the rest of the war, and the ships were released for other military service. The better-off civilians particularly missed the *Royal Edward*, which kept its first, second and third class cabins, the better of which could be rented at between 2 shillings and 5 shillings a week. It was an extraordinary arrangement but one that impressed the American ambassador to Berlin when the Germans asked him to visit Britain to inspect prisoner-of-war facilities. A 'ship of show' was his verdict on the *Royal Edward*.

Not, alas, for much longer. Newly restored as a troop carrier, a function she had carried out in the earliest days of the war, she left Avonmouth in late July 1915 with 1,367 officers and men bound for Gallipoli, most of them reinforcements for the British 29th Infantry, along with members of the Royal Army Medical Corps. On 13 August, homing in on the Dardanelles, she was struck by two torpedoes launched from a German submarine, and sank in six minutes with the loss of more than 900 lives. The *Ivernia* suffered a similar fate off Cape Matapan in Greece on the morning of New Year's Day 1917, with 120 killed, but the *Saxonia*, built on the Clyde in 1899 and the oldest of the three, survived troop transport duties unscathed and was even converted back to civilian use, at considerable expense, before being scrapped in 1925.

For both the ships and their residents, then, Christmas 1914 was a one-off, a rare season of goodwill at a time when such sentiments were in short supply. Looking back today, perhaps most touching of all is the faith in the international postal system and the integrity of the British authorities shown by those families and friends back in Germany who sent off their cakes, cigars and chocolates in the confident belief that they would reach their menfolk promptly and intact. They did, and on one level that is a feel-good legacy almost as remarkable as the Christmas Day truce at the front.

# 'MY OWN LITTLE BOY
IS IN THE HOSPITAL
WITH DIPHTHERIA'

The epidemic most readily identified with the First World War was the influenza pandemic, which lasted throughout the three years from 1918 to 1920. It infected 500 million people, from remote Pacific islands to the Arctic Circle, and was famously more deadly than the war by far by claiming anything up to 100 million victims. As censors played down its effects on the major warring countries, including Britain, Germany, France and the United States, it became known as Spanish flu, as reports on its impact in that neutral country circulated far more freely.

Not so headline-grabbing but an abiding and demoralising presence throughout the war was diphtheria, the upper respiratory illness which had a particularly lethal effect on children. Like the influenza outbreak of 1918, its spread was exacerbated by the conditions of war; the spread of flu was aided by the constant movement of young adults and the undernourishment, stress and generally run-down state of health of so many of them, while untreated diphtheria will flourish in insanitary, overcrowded and wretched living conditions. That was a way of life known by all too many people at that time.

We now know that in the Western world, at least, immunisation has transformed diphtheria from a mass killer to a disease that can be kept under control. A pioneer in this was Emil Adolf von Behring, a German physiologist who in 1901 won the first Nobel Prize in Physiology or Medicine for developing antitoxin serum therapies against diphtheria, which he improved and refined on the eve of the First World War. Work by him and others had seen a steady fall in cases for about thirty years up until the war, but they increased sharply during the hostilities and stayed high until around 1931, when the level started to fall. Nevertheless, even in the Second World War diphtheria grew into the most prevalent infectious disease in Western Europe, and the most common one contracted by servicemen of most of the conflicting armies.

Its devastating effect on life and morale in the First World War is encapsulated in the story of the family of Private William Workman of the 3rd (Special Reserve) Battalion of the Gloucestershire Regiment. He was killed by a sniper at nine o' clock on Christmas morning on a section of the front in France where the festive spirit evidently did not prevail – but almost simultaneously, one of his five little children at home in Stroud died of diphtheria. As if this were not tragic enough, the Gloucestershire Regiment NCO who wrote a kind, thoughtful letter of sympathy to Private Workman's widow, revealed that he could quite understand her sense of loss at the death of her husband, as he himself had a child at home suffering from diphtheria. Writing from the front, he would not, of course, have had any inkling of the loss of the Workman child – but the coincidence of both these parents suffering the anguish of this deadly illness in their children, on top of everything else that the war was throwing at them, is a reminder of the grinding, unremitting sadness suffered by so many people at that dreadful time. Colour Sergeant A. Mayall's letter read as follows:

> I deeply regret having to inform you that your dear husband died of a wound received on Christmas Day. He was struck by a stray bullet about nine o'clock and passed peacefully away during the afternoon. How much I feel for you words cannot say, as I can fully appreciate and share your feelings, for my own little boy is in the hospital with diphtheria. We shall miss your husband very much, as he has been in my company since we left England. He always did his duty nobly and well, and was cheerful even under the most trying circumstances.
>
> We are all hoping this terrible war will soon cease, but duty has called us in defence of our homes and loved ones, and our brave men will not have given their lives in vain as our object must soon be, with God's help, accomplished, and a lasting peace ensured.

On behalf of the men of the company, I beg to offer you
our most heartfelt sympathy in your great sorrow and
loss. Bear up, and try to endure your sad loss with this
to cheer: He died in the performance of his duty which,
as I said before, was always most nobly performed by him.

Whether or not Mrs Workman was much uplifted by
this last sentiment, we shall never know. But when
she sat down to read the letter for the hundredth
time, Colour Sergeant Mayall's anxiety over his son's
diphtheria must surely have struck a chord with her,
along with the humanity and thoughtfulness of his
words, sent from a place of previously undreamed-of
death and destruction. They would certainly have
contrasted notably with the official War Office letter
notifying her of her husband's death, a brief docu-
ment that became notorious for its brusqueness and
lack of sympathy.

# MERCY
# DISGUISED
# BY MOCKERY

Josef Tomann was an Austrian junior doctor who
spent the first Christmas of the war in the garrison hospital at Przemysl in Poland, where the
Austria-Hungarian forces had been besieged by
the advancing Russians since October. His diary
entries over the holiday period are remarkable for
several reasons, not least for their account of the
rough-and-ready spirit of goodwill shown by the
Russian troops at grassroots level; it is not, after
all, the role of a besieging army to point their
beleaguered enemy towards free food and then
grant them safe access to it. It was lack of supplies,
however, coupled with illness and exhaustion, that
saw the fortress surrender in March 1915, when the
Russians destroyed all its defences and rendered it of
no strategic importance, temporarily, at least. It is
estimated that during the fighting around Przemysl,
both sides lost up to 115,000 killed, wounded
or missing.

An *Illustrated War News* artist's impression of Russian and
Austria-Hungarian troops fighting hand-to-hand at Przemysl.
Casualties were indeed horrific, but it was the sheer, grinding
misery of siege conditions that eventually led the Austrians to
surrender. (*The Illustrated War News*, 13 January 1915)

Tomann's account of that horrific Christmas is
taken from the book *A War In Words* in which Svetlana
Palmer and Sarah Wallis took diaries and letters written by twenty-eight men and women and wove them
into a powerful and immediate account of everyday life
in the First World War. The collection is particularly
valuable as it enters theatres of war far beyond the
Western Front, although that is there, too. The Eastern
Front, the Dardanelles, the mountainous front between
Italy and Austria-Hungary and East Africa are all areas
to which little thought is being given in Britain in the
centenary year of 2014, yet they are brought vividly to
life in Palmer and Wallis's book.

**THE UNWELCOME CHRISTMAS VISITOR.**

The Kaiser (desperately): "Can't you push him back, Hindenburg?—he's coming in!"

The Russians pushing in the door on the Kaiser and Hindenburg in Silesia. In the First World War cartoonists quickly had to learn to portray the Bear as resolute and determined, rather than hostile and snarling. (*The War Pictures Weekly*, 31 December 1914)

December 24

It is Christmas Eve and I'm here on my own in a hostile country. I cannot rest today, my weary mind is troubled by dreams and sweet visions that fill the air like phantoms. When we were children we looked forward to Christmas Eve with great excitement. It was a time we always spent with our dear mother, but she will be on her own today crying over her three sons away at war.

Else was born this year. It was only last summer that Mitzl and I talked about how lovely it would be to have our first Christmas together. But we couldn't decide where to spend it. The war has made that decision for us. What is it like this year at home, I wonder? Do the lights on the tree twinkle as brightly? Sister Victoria showed me the Christmas tree, sprinkled with chalk and decorated with a few small candles. The poor chaps will be glad. I don't want to see or hear anything – I'll stay at home and try in vain to bury myself in a book. And yet twice I have felt hot tears on my cheeks. The war and its miseries have hardened me. Why am I so pathetic today? We cry every year, but this year we cry bitter tears.

Dr Friedmann has a fever of 30.5. Typhoid perhaps. Dr Weiszt has influenza. Niemcow is still sick.

### December 26

On Christmas morning our scouts found three Christmas trees the Russians had left in no-man's-land with notes that said something like 'We wish you, the heroes of Przemysl, a Merry Christmas, and hope that we can come to a peaceful agreement as soon as possible.' There was a truce on Christmas Day, they neither attacked nor fired.

### December 31

The Russian soldiers make a neighing sound whenever they see our troops, as they know we are forced to eat horse meat in the fortress. A few days ago one of our patrols found a note they'd left us, showing where the potato and cabbage fields were and saying they would stop shooting while we fetched some food. It was true! When our soldiers went over, the Russians shot two blanks high into the air, just to let them know they'd seen them. The next day we all went for more.

It's the last day of the year! I shan't be sorry to see the back of 1914. On the other hand, I was so happy with my dear Mitzl for seven months of the year, and on 7th June 1914 Else came into the world! I am contented, I ask for nothing more.

The worst of the war is certainly behind us. We are now moving towards peace. Peace – the idea seems almost alien to me. Will it come soon? Then I can devote myself to my family and my job. The hope that next year will see us reunited with our loved ones is what keeps us going. It gives me the heart and strength for the coming year. Onwards, I am ready!

# From footlights to trenches

New Year 1915 brought the first showbiz tour to the troops at the front, an idea that must have seemed revolutionary at the time, not least because of the cast list. It included two of the great pin-ups of the day, Gladys Cooper and (the admittedly slightly ageing) Ellaline Terriss, both stars of the musical comedies that had dominated the West End stage in the pre-war years. Soldier's wife Gladys went on to be the great British forces sweetheart of the First World War, and this genuinely plucky step into the unknown must have played a part in that.

The shows, which also visited hospitals close to the front, were organised by Seymour Hicks, an actor and impresario who was a showbiz household name from the late 1880s into the 1940s. He called the tour 'The National Theatre At The Front', although it predated today's National Theatre by all but fifty years. Ellaline Terriss was his wife. Another headliner was the Welsh tenor Ben Davies, while a further solid

Gladys Cooper, whose career spanned from the 1890s to the 1960s, but was never more high profile than in the early years of the twentieth century. (Author's collection)

name on the bill was the musical comedy actress Ivy
St Helier, a Channel Islander like Hicks; her biggest
day would come years later when she played Manon
'la Crevette' in the original production of Noël
Coward's *Bitter Sweet* in 1929, and reprised the role
in the 1933 film.

For the Scots troops in particular came Willie Frame,
a comedian who was all but unintelligible to audiences from south of the border. The flautist Eli Hudson,
former principal flute with the London Symphony
Orchestra but now more at home in the halls, was
on the trip with his pianist sister Olga, usually known
off-stage as Winnie, leaving their harmonium-playing
sister Elgar at home. Will Van Allen was there with
his cheery chatter and his banjo, the instrument for
which he is still best remembered today; he gave his
name to a brand of banjos and sundry instruments,
and George Formby was an early admirer of his ban-
joleles, if that does not sound too much like a Formby
double entendre. The party was completed by a
cinema projectionist whose task was not eased by the
filthy conditions in which he was called upon to work.

The group left Victoria railway station in London
in the early afternoon of Sunday, 27 December,
and returned the following weekend. They departed
'amid hearty demonstrations from a considerable gathering' that included Arthur Playfair, at the height of
his career in West End musical comedies and revues,
and the elderly actor-manager Sir Squire Bancroft.

Hicks's aim was to hit the ground running and put on three shows at military hospitals in Boulogne that evening.

*The War Budget* weekly was overwhelmed by the venture. 'Surely a tour of the trenches by popular London footlight favourites must be a unique record in this unique war!' it declared.

Yet Mr Seymour Hicks and a number of other well-known actors and actresses are giving variety entertainments to soldiers at the front, having all kinds of hardships and discomforts in a splendid effort to cheer the lads who are fighting in the greatest war the Empire has ever been called upon to wage.

The tour is being made, of course, by permission of the French military authorities, and the performances are being given in the open air, under canvas or even, if need be, in the 'dug-outs'. The programme will consist of songs, sketches, and the cinematograph – a typical variety bill, in fact, only without the customary playlet of the 'thrill' sort. It would be carrying coals to Newcastle to take 'thrills' to the boys at the front. With regard to the cinematograph, the party will show comic pictures only – ten thousand feet of funny films. The sketches are 'Always Tell Your Wife' and 'The Bridal Suite'. Mr Seymour Hicks appears with his wife in the first and with Miss Gladys Cooper in the second. He has specially chosen these sketches for performance because they require little or no scenery – just a table and a chair or two, which may possibly be packing cases at that. Two portable pianos will make up the 'orchestra'. Miss Ellaline Terriss sings her recent Coliseum repertoire of songs, including her new version of 'A Little Bit Of String', the last verse of which, with its reference to a certain foreign celebrity, will no doubt be highly appreciated. Old English songs will be contributed to the entertainment by that fine vocalist Mr Ben Davies.

The songs will be sung, and parts played, in the rough, warm clothes of travel. The party will go where they are told, do whatever they are asked by the military authorities, provide their own motors and food, and will aim at doing as much good and giving as little trouble as possible.

They were undoubtedly a showbizzy bunch, and it is a shame we do not know more about how their efforts went down; if there was a show on New Year's Eve, for example, it must have been a lively gathering. What does still exist is a playbill they produced for the tour, well-meaning but full of the kind of gushing false modesty to which theatre people can still fall prey today:

Fellow countrymen of whom we are so proud, and to whom we owe so much ... We, your brothers and sisters, have come over from England to try and entertain and amuse you during New Year's Week, and bring you 'A MESSAGE FROM HOME'. You have only to command us and we shall be proud to give you the best entertainment in our power AT ANY TIME AND AT ANY PLACE ...

HERE WE ARE! HERE WE ARE! HERE WE ARE AGAIN!
IT'S A LONG, LONG WAY TO TIPPERARY, BUT NOT TOO
FAR FOR US, BLESS YOU!!! You will confer a favour on
us by letting us work for you, and the angels in disguise,
the brave ladies who nurse you, ask them to honour us
with their presence also. GOD SAVE THE KING. GOD
PROTECT YOU AND YOUR BRAVE ALLIES! LONG LIVE
ENGLAND! VIVE LA FRANCE! BRAVO, BRAVE BELGIUM!
The price of admission is £ OUR GRATITUDE TO YOU.

Some of the brief pen-pictures after the artists' name
have a certain appeal. 'Ellaline Terriss will sing more
sweetly and act more charmingly than ever for you'
is followed instantly by 'Seymour Hicks will perspire
more freely', as indeed he had every reason to do. After
'Ben Davies will sing as he never sang before' comes
'Gladys Cooper will act and look more like her postcards
than they do', a quirky nod towards her A-list fame.

It is interesting that *The War Budget* referred in its
piece to 'variety', rather than 'music hall'. Since the
London Pavilion was rebuilt in 1885 many, though
by no means all, theatre operators had been trying
to throw off the beery, rough-and-ready image of
the original dives and take the shows up market.
Architects such as Frank Matcham grew rich and
famous designing great marble and gilded temples to
reflect the new order, and the journey to respectability
was complete when George V attended the first Royal
Variety Performance at the Palace Theatre in London

Your humble servants:
the concert party's playbill
as displayed in field hospitals.
(Author's collection)

in 1912. Seymour Hicks and his cohorts were indeed
from the variety end of the market, while many of
the lads in their audiences in France would have been
more at home in small-town music halls. One and all
would doubtless have enjoyed the rubbishing of Kaiser
Bill, the 'certain foreign celebrity' of Ellaline's song.

As *The War Budget*'s report suggests, the artists were
left very much to their own devices; and as the buck
stopped with the Hickses, it is perhaps not surprising
that they were declared bankrupt, though briefly,
shortly after the party returned home in 1915. In truth,

their finances were by no means sound before the trip, because while they dazzled on stage, they had come disastrously unstuck a decade earlier through their part in building three at first unsuccessful new theatres, including the Aldwych. Not that their careers were by any means on the rocks: although musical comedy was past its peak they remained headliners for two decades after the war in comedy revues and variety, Hicks wrote and produced several new shows and his film career included an acclaimed performance as Scrooge in the 1935 film of that name, the first sound version of Dickens's *A Christmas Carol*. Some critics say that though later eclipsed by Alastair Sim's interpretation, Hicks's is closer to the character that Dickens portrayed.

Seymour and Ellaline Hicks were in their early 40s by 1914, so she was not quite the stunning beauty she had been in the 1890s or indeed in 1902, when the General Post Office had sparked the picture postcard craze by allowing both address and message to be written on one side, freeing the other for an illustration. She was one of the first great postcard pin-ups, and the luminously beautiful Gladys Cooper, who had been a child model from the age of 6, was another. She celebrated her twenty-sixth birthday at the trenches, while her first husband, Captain Herbert Buckmaster of the Royal Horse Guards, was somewhere else out there.

Hicks's efforts at the front won him the Croix de Guerre from the French, but it is unknown how much this considerable venture contributed to his knighthood in 1934. Most would accept that if it is right to reward theatre people with such honours, Hicks had probably earned one twice over through his other efforts alone. It was as old stagers that he and Ellaline returned to the front in the Second World War, this time with Entertainments National Service Association doing all the organising and picking up the bills. Nevertheless, the ever-grateful French thought his contribution was worth another Croix de Guerre.

Even in 1914 the tenor Ben Davies was in his mid-50s, but from what he told *The London Illustrated Weekly*, he enjoyed his experiences in France. His had been a long and successful career in operas and oratorios, but in his recordings he and his management had seen commercial sense in adding popular parlour songs to his repertoire: after all, they were easy for him to sing, and they were what the public liked. He told the magazine that he had returned from the trenches with, if possible, an increased admiration for the British Tommy: 'He is the finest fellow in the world. Brave in action and patient in suffering and seeing humour in everything. Even those lying in hospital take their knock-down with a shrug and a jest.' The singer added that his Welsh songs were particularly popular with his fellow countrymen, but 'Sally In Our Alley' had gone down best of all, followed by 'To Mary', 'My Dreams' and 'Songs of Araby'. On the other hand, he had put all of these out on record in recent times, so maybe there was some cunning product placement going on here.

A footnote: both Ellaline Terriss, from a notable showbiz dynasty, and Gladys Cooper lived on well into the second half of the twentieth century. Fifty years after the trenches show, Dame Gladys crowned a versatile career on stage and in film and television with an Oscar nomination for her role as Professor Higgins's mother in the movie of *My Fair Lady*. She died in Henley-on-Thames in November 1971, aged 82. Ellaline had died just five months earlier, but her film career had ended in 1939 and she had not been on stage since the death of her husband in 1949. A long spell out of the spotlight, then – but trouper that she was, she enjoyed one last curtain call by celebrating her hundredth birthday and being feted with flowers and greetings at a Hampstead nursing home in the April, before dying after a fall two months later.

Ellaline Terriss, who with her husband Seymour Hicks travelled to the front to entertain the troops in both world wars. (Author's collection)

# BIBLIOGRAPHY

Arthur, Max, *Forgotten Voices of the Great War* (Ebury Press, 2003)

Briggs, Asa, *A Social History of England* (Penguin, 1986)

Cameron, James, *1914* (Cassell, 1969)

Crozier, F.P., *A Brass Hat in No Man's Land* (Jonathan Cape, 1937)

Eyre, Giles E.M., *Somme Harvest: Memories of a PBI in the summer of 1916* (Naval and Military Press, 2001)

Hollis, Matthew, *Now All Roads Lead To France: The last years of Edward Thomas* (Faber and Faber, 2011)

Hudson, John, *A Cotswold Christmas* (Alan Sutton Publishing, 1988)

MacArthur, Brian (ed.), *For King and Country: Voices from the First World War* (Little, Brown Book Group, 2008)

Marsay, Mark, *Bombardment: The Day the East Coast Bled* (Great Northern Publishing, 1999)

Moore, John, *The Life and Letters of Edward Thomas* (William Heinemann, 1939)

Palmer, Svetlana and Sarah Wallis (eds), *A War in Words: The First World War in Diaries and Letters* (Simon & Schuster UK, 2003, reprinted 2014)

Paxman, Jeremy, *Great Britain's Great War* (Viking, 2013)

Riddock, Andrew and John Kemp, *When The Whistle Blows: The story of the Footballers' Battalion in the Great War* (Haynes Publishing, 2008)

Rutt, Richard, *A History of Hand Knitting* (Batsford, 1987)

Thurston, Violetta, *Field Hospital And Flying Column: Being the journal of an English nursing sister in Belgium and Russia* (G.P. Putnam's Sons, London and New York, 1915, with later reprints by Kessinger Publishing, Leonaur, Nabu Press, Rarebooksclub.com et al)

Weintraub, Stanley, *Silent Night: The remarkable 1914 Christmas Truce* (Simon & Schuster, 2001)

## Papers and Journals

*Picture And Story*, published by the *Amalgamated Press*

*The Illustrated War News*, Parts 13–24, 4 November 1914–20 January 1915

*The London Illustrated Weekly*, 1 October 1914–11 February 1915

*The Penny War Weekly*, 5 September 1914–3 January 1915, amalgamated as *The War In 'Vivid'*

*The War Budget*, 21 November 1914–13 February 1915, published by *The Daily Chronicle*

*T.P.'s Journal Of Great Deeds Of The Great War*, 17 October 1914–9 January 1915

## Websites

www.1914-1918.net
www.bbc.co.uk/news
www.bradford-theatres.co.uk
www.bradfordww1.co.uk
www.christmastruce.co.uk
www.crossingthewhiteline.com
www.dartfordarchive.org.uk
www.doubleeagleclub.org
www.dover.freeuk.com/war/ww1.htm

www.dover-kent.co.uk/history/ww1c_bombing.htm
www.fleetairarmoa.org
www.firstworldwar.com/features
http://forums.catholic.com
www.history.com/topics/world-war-i
www.historylearningsite.co.uk
www.historyofwar.org
www.kenthistoryforum.co.uk
www.kinnethmont.co.uk/1914-1918_files/xmas-box-1914.htm
www.likeyoudo.org.uk/gwmc
www.marksheridan.org
www.pigstrough.co.uk/ww1
www.scarboroughsmaritimeheritage.org.uk
www.scottishgolfhistory.org/origin-of-golf-terms/bogey
www.societyforpeace.org.uk
www.spartacus.schoolnet.co.uk/FWWtull.htm
www.tamworthherald.co.uk
www.thisishartlepool.co.uk/history
www.victoriacross.org.uk/bbholbro.htm
www.waltertull.com
www.westernfrontassociation.com
www.wingsofwar.org